MANAGE YOURSELF, MANAGE YOUR LIFE

IAN McDERMOTT and
IAN SHIRCORE

MANAGE YOURSELF, MANAGE YOUR LIFE

Vital NLP techniques for
personal well-being and
professional success

PIATKUS

First published in the UK by
Judy Piatkus (Publishers) Limited
5 Windmill Street
London W1P 1HF
e-mail: info@piatkus.co.uk

The moral rights of the authors have been asserted

*A catalogue record for this book is available
from the British Library*

ISBN 0 7499 1990 6

Page design by Sue Ryall
Edited by Carol Franklin

Set by Action Publishing Technology, Gloucester
Digitally printed by Butler and Tanner
Burgess Hill, West Sussex

For Paulette
who manages life on two continents

and for

Molly Elliott Shircore,
who has a gift for squaring circles

Contents

PART THREE   To Manage is to Live

PART I

The Secrets of NLP

Chapter 1

A New Sense of Control

*Life is yours to make sense of and its value is the
sense you choose to make.*

Jean-Paul Sartre

Why manage?

Because you can do more, live more, be more. Because it's more
fun. Because you owe it to yourself to be the author of your own
life story. Because work and business are a waste of time if they
don't give you what you need. Because you could be happier.
And healthier. And richer.

How many reasons do you need?

Because it's better to be the doer than the done. Because life's
more interesting than drifting. Because other people will always
tell you what you're supposed to be doing, but only you know
what you must do. Because families don't always work in your
favour. Because bad luck happens. Because you deserve the

chance to show what you can do. Because you don't want to be blaming other people.

Managing your life doesn't mean controlling every aspect of it, or trying to bend reality to conform to some great master plan. But it does mean acknowledging that most of what is good in your life is likely to come from or be enhanced by what is good and positive within you. Your career, your relationships and your day-to-day habits of thinking and behaviour can all be heavily influenced by the choices you make.

This book is a practical guide to making the most of yourself, your home and work situations, and the things that are happening around you.

It will help you become clearer, in your own mind, about what you really want and what your priorities are. It will also help you sharpen up your mental and physical fitness, so that you feel more robust and more resilient – and more able emotionally to deal with whatever life throws at you.

This is not a book about long-term navel-gazing, nor about kidding yourself that things are good when they are not. Withdrawing into a world of dreams is something we can all get a lot of value from every night, but our days have to be lived out there in the rough-and-tumble of the external world. This is the world of homes and families, jobs and money, children and elderly people, cars and bills, birth, sex, death and TV. What we make of all this is what we make of our lives.

All you need for a personal revolution

For most people, the extra assets that would be most helpful in living day-to-day life to the full would not be superhuman strength or incredible brainpower. What we need is more energy, so that we can tackle our days with verve and inexhaustible enthusiasm, and more resourcefulness, so that when things don't go to plan we can quickly come up with ingenious alternatives and other ways of achieving our goals.

But energy isn't a purely physical matter – and resourcefulness is not all in the mind. Your inability to get stuck in to a job you have been putting off for days is more likely to be a question of how you feel about it than whether or not you have the strength or stamina for it. A very slight adjustment to the way you approach the task may be all you need to get it humming along nicely.

Take the example of filling in tax forms. They are essentially complex, hostile documents, aren't they, with dozens of difficult and intrusive questions to answer? How could anyone not hate the chore of completing them? But have you ever had the experience of filling in one of these forms, knowing that once it is submitted you will eventually receive a tax rebate? Admittedly, it's a rare occurrence. But it is amazing how different the process seems, when apprehension is set aside and you know the arithmetic is coming out in your favour. Same forms. Same questions, even. But just knowing that all these figures and calculations are going to end up with the tax office owing you money changes the whole perspective. And when the perspective changes, everything changes.

This book is for everyone who is prepared to accept the simple truth that success, happiness and fulfilment begin on the inside. And what is on the inside is always, at least partially, under your control. If you are prepared to read and learn a number of straightforward techniques that will help you manage yourself inside, we can guarantee that you will be able to manage your life better and enjoy more of what you want and need, both personally and professionally. This is our promise – and we won't let you down.

By showing you in quite specific detail how you can manage

your own personal resources better – and how you can extend that sense of choice and control out into your work and your relationships – this book can give you all the ammunition you need for a personal revolution.

If you are not yet ready for a revolution, this book can give you access to a range of insights and techniques for taking control of your life and staying in command when things feel rocky, or when doubt and inertia threaten to get the better of you.

The insights and advice here have been drawn together from many sources, including our own professional and personal experiences, and the findings of scientists and academics in many different fields of study. Between the two of us, we have over thirty years' practical experience in management and marketing consultancy projects, including crucial problem-solving work for blue-chip corporations in areas such as energy, telecoms, computing, shipping and publishing. In addition, one of us, Ian McDermott, has twenty years' experience as a psychotherapist, enabling people to make the changes they want in their lives. But what gives the book its unique flavour is the strong influence of NLP – neurolinguistic programming – that underpins most of the content.

How can NLP help you?

As the name implies, neurolinguistic programming is a synthesis that draws on the work of a number of different disciplines, with a special emphasis on linguistics and the neurosciences. It is about exploring and explaining how human beings really work and finding ways to help people use that knowledge. In particular, NLP has looked at many ways of changing limiting patterns of behaviour and enhancing those patterns to work in our favour. This is a vital area of study, because these patterns account for a lot of the oddities of human actions and reactions. Whether they work for us or against us, we all have our own habitual sequences of behaviour that we run through completely automatically. These are the programmes that can be changed and enriched using the techniques of neurolinguistic programming.

It has taken more than a quarter of a century for NLP to grow from its trial-and-error experimental phase in California in the 1970s into the fertile, tried-and-tested approach and methodology that is now being embraced by top management in many major corporations.

The movement into the mainstream is hard to quantify, but our own private research has confirmed that at least eighteen of the top thirty companies listed on the London Stock Exchange have worked with NLP trainers or consultants, as well as European multinationals such as Fiat, Nestlé, Volkswagen and Siemens and a host of America's business leaders. This is not fringe science any more. Many of NLP's early findings have been incorporated, in diluted form, into today's standard management training. No one is surprised to see these training programmes laying emphasis on the elements of personal rapport, such as the importance of being in synch with another person and the possibility of achieving this through a subtle approximation of their body language, energy levels, posture and gestures. Yet this is pure NLP. In the same way, being able to identify and work with people's preferred communication styles – visual or auditory, for example – has become a recognised business skill, even if it is often airily dismissed as 'just common sense'. This is NLP, too – and far from just common sense.

The danger is that these borrowings from NLP may be seen as bolt-on extras, by people who pick them up in second-hand forms and never come to realise how much more they could be gaining. This is a major concern for Ian McDermott, who has been actively involved for many years in the continuing devel-

opment of NLP and who runs one of the world's leading NLP-
based training and business consultancy groups, International
Teaching Seminars, as well as lecturing and training in both
Europe and America. He and Ian Shircore, who makes his living
writing about business and management issues, from team
building to the Internet, are dedicated to the idea of bringing
'real' NLP to a far wider audience.

In our previous book together (*NLP and the New Manager*,
Orion Business Books 1998), we focused specifically on introducing a broad range of business applications of NLP. This time
the aim is even more ambitious – to produce a book that will
help you achieve change and take control of all the key aspects
of your life, when you want to, in your own way and at your
own pace.

For many ordinary people, with lives to lead and jobs to do,
but no great business decisions to make or high-stakes negotiations to conduct, the idea of developing the kind of fine-tuned
goal-setting and communications skills that are so highly valued
in corporate management may seem slightly incongruous. But
these skills, which come with a knowledge of NLP, can be
applied in a vast range of contexts and situations. What could
be more important than the negotiations between a parent and
a teenager about buying a motorbike or staying out all night or
travelling overland to somewhere far away? These things matter
enormously if you are one of the people concerned. They could
even become matters of life and death, if you take a cold-eyed
view of all the possible consequences. So it is hugely important
that family decisions and debates like this are taken seriously
and treated with all the skills that can be brought to bear on
them.

In the real world, of course, it matters a great deal more if a
hotheaded youngster is injured in a crash on his first motorbike
than if the national marketing campaign for some minor electronic product fails to make the expected impact. The ability of

business to overrate its relatively puny importance in the true scheme of things is one of the reasons so many second-rate managers fail to understand and motivate their staff. What happens to you, your family and your friends is so much more important to you than any set of figures on a balance sheet. Similarly, on a day-to-day basis what is going on in your relationships often sets the tone of your life, making you feel happy, lively, relaxed and productive – or, on bad days, edgy, tired, sad and at sixes and sevens with the world around you.

Even business always comes down to people

The fact that NLP's lessons, insights and practical advice can be applied equally well at home and at work makes them doubly useful. The artificial divide between life and work and between people's home and work personalities is something that we'll touch on later. But the truth is there are few work decisions that are really taken on a wholly factual, dispassionate, Spock-like basis. Every sales trainee soon learns that, even in business-to-business markets, you don't sell to companies, you sell to people. So the skills of rapid rapport-building, vividly convincing communication and even, most fundamentally of all, knowing what you really want, are just as essential in the salesroom and the boardroom as they are in the wine bar and the bedroom.

Spontaneous excellence is lovely when it happens. Everyone knows that fantastic feeling you get on those great days when the force is with you and you couldn't go wrong if you tried. These are the days when things are the way they should be and your personal relationships are easy and loving. If you're working, the problems just melt away in front of you. If you're playing sport, you can effortlessly perform beyond the limits of your normal capabilities. If you're painting or writing or studying, you're absorbed in the flow, full of relaxed, productive concentration that makes you wonder why you ever stared with gritted teeth at an empty canvas or a blank sheet of paper and felt you would never progress again.

It's a great feeling. The only problem is arranging your life so that you are always on this kind of transcendentally wonderful form when it will do you the most good. On the days when you're not, you need a bit of technique to help you through.

Throughout this book, we will be focusing your attention on some of the ways you can use simple NLP techniques to bring more of your life back under your own control. We will also be looking at how you can manage the key aspects of your life involved with health, wealth and relationships, work and happiness, and at how you can make the most of the turning points when something significant changes in your life.

There's a limit to what you can control

First, though, it is important to sort out exactly what we mean when we talk about managing your life and exercising control over what happens to you and around you. It's certainly not a matter of believing that just a bit more power and a bit more control over other people and external events would give you security, happiness and everything you could wish for. There are a great many external factors bearing on your life and your work which are beyond all human control. People who keep swearing at the weather for not being kinder to them have problems that are more than just meteorological.

This book is not about managing the totally unmanageable nor controlling things that, by their nature, are not amenable to control. But it is concerned with breaking some of the links between events that are beyond our control and our reactions to them. These reactions could, potentially, be controlled and managed.

If Lisa acts in a certain way and Mark becomes angry, you may say that Lisa infuriates Mark – but it is important to understand that what is going on is not a simple matter of cause and effect. Saying that Lisa infuriates Mark is not the same as saying that Lisa tickles Mark, or hits him, or picks him up by the scruff of his neck and throws him across the room. Those are actions she does to him. When she infuriates him, that is not strictly something she does to him. She acts; he reacts. But there is not an unbreakable chain of cause and effect here.

In fact, infuriating though Lisa's actions may seem, Mark may choose not to be angered by them. He may say: 'Come on – I think you've had enough for one evening. Let me get your coat.' He may laugh and say: 'Stop it, you. I'm not going to rise to the bait that easily.' Or he may be genuinely infuriated and storm out, looking homicidal and muttering that he never wants to see her again. The important point here is that Mark's reaction is ultimately under his control, not Lisa's.

One of the central strengths of NLP is its emphasis on people's responsibility for their own reactions. 'You make me angry' is seen as an essentially misleading statement. 'You do this and I get angry' is nearer the truth, because, ultimately, nobody makes *me* angry but *me*.

No one is saying that people should not be angry, or that they should pretend not to be angry and bottle up their feelings. It may be absolutely appropriate for Mark to feel angry and even to feel that his relationship with Lisa is at an end. He is probably disappointed, irritated, appalled and maybe even disgusted. But that is his privilege and those are his feelings. However upset he feels at the time, it is simply not true that Lisa has disappointed, irritated, appalled and disgusted him, because all those shades of feeling depend very largely on the way he has chosen to interpret the situation. They are inside him, rather than objective realities floating about in the air around the stressed-out couple. On another day, in another mood, he would react differently to exactly the same sequence of events. That is the proof that the link between Lisa's actions and his reaction is not a matter of fact, but a matter of feeling. And if Mark decides it is in his interests to control and manage his response, NLP can teach him how.

Choose how you feel – association and dissociation

If you are not used to thinking in these terms, just realising how often you can exercise a choice about how you will react to particular events can be quite a breakthrough in itself.

You really do have a lot more choice about how you feel and what you take from the situation, in all sorts of circumstances, than people usually realise. For example, if you take up hiking or running, camping, sailing, gardening, walking a dog or cycling to work, you soon notice the way your relationship with the weather changes. You start to want different things from the weather or to appreciate different aspects of it.

Instead of looking out through a window or a windscreen and classifying the day as good (meaning dry, warm and bright) or bad (meaning dull, wet, windy, cold, misty or snowy), you start to notice more of the subtleties of the weather and respond to it in less extreme ways. If you want to enjoy your sailing, a bit of wind does no harm at all. Marathon runners do not wake up to blazing sunshine and think 'Great – just the weather for 26 miles 384 yards and topping up my tan.' They prefer a cool, overcast day, with perhaps a light drizzle. And even if what you do doesn't demand a particular sort of weather, you can find unexpected pleasure in quite unpromising conditions. Dog owners might not look forward to going out in the rain, but most will admit that a brisk walk on a mild, wet, blustery morning can be surprisingly energising, if you just let yourself take it as it comes and enjoy it.

The ability to be open and receptive like this, so that you can enjoy things you are not expecting to enjoy, is a talent that is worth nurturing – and one you can develop quite easily. This book will give you several techniques that will help you do it. You can make a start right now, just by deciding to surprise yourself with sudden pleasure spot-checks during the day. As soon as you begin doing this, your brain will quickly cotton on to the idea that it may be quizzed, at any time, about what's going on and how receptive it is being. And just knowing this will make a difference you can feel. You can begin the process straight away, without any preparation. Sometime soon, just pause for a moment and ask yourself two simple questions:

1. What is enjoyable about what I am doing, what I feel or what is going on around me?
2. If it is enjoyable, am I letting myself make the most of it?

Ideally, to get full value from the enjoyable aspects of what you are experiencing, you will want to be as engaged and involved as possible, living in the moment and relishing what it has to offer. In the same way, there will be other times when unpleasant things are happening and you will want to be as abstracted, remote, dissociated and uninvolved as you can possibly be.

This is partly a matter of technique. For example, to make the most of an enjoyable situation, you will want to immerse yourself in it at the sensory level, taking in all the sights, sounds, feelings and smells and being fully aware of the input from each of these sense channels. You will want to lap up the experience and savour it, feeling it fully.

At the other extreme, in the sort of situation where you just wish you were a hundred miles away, you need to switch from the feeling channel to seeing things from another point of view – literally. Some people have had the experience of being in a car that they could see was about to impact another and finding themselves quite spontaneously looking down on the whole scene as if from above. This is a natural human ability that very effectively reduces our involvement and the feelings that would otherwise go with it.

This ability to dissociate can be extremely useful on occasion. You can do it in different ways. Concentrate on analysing a particular aspect of what is going on, in order to engage the thinking brain, rather than the centres of feeling and emotion. Try to pick out a pattern, think of a parallel or remember something like this that happened to someone else. Think of a pop song that would be an apt soundtrack to the situation – or a famous quotation that would fit the bill. But by far the most powerful way is to change your point of view, step outside the action and watch it unfold from a disembodied, fly-on-the-wall perspective.

These basic techniques of association and dissociation will help give you more choices. They will become valuable tools in your self-management toolkit and help you decide for yourself how you want to react in exciting, unexpected or threatening situations.

All you need to do is start practising each technique so that you can use them at will:

1. To get better at associating, start paying more attention to the feeling dimension. One easy way to do this is to start noticing how your body feels and then to give yourself more of what makes you feel good. This gives you a good reason for feeling what you're feeling.

2. To improve your ability to dissociate, start stepping

outside situations so you can see yourself from the point of view of a spectator. You'll find it gives you a quite different perspective on situations that is extremely useful.

Control means starting things (as well as stopping things)

One of the most important points to make about managing yourself and managing your life is that managing should not be seen as restricting or diminishing. The aim of this book is certainly not to help you achieve iron self-discipline as a route to success and happiness. In fact, there doesn't seem to be much evidence that either hell-for-leather hedonism or stringent self-denial are particularly effective recipes for success, in a business context or in life. Complete self-indulgence and complete self-restraint are both pretty unattractive to outsiders. What's more, they don't generally seem to do their exponents much good in the long term.

This book will help you to achieve your best. And because life is so full of stray threads, loose ends and unforeseen diversions, an improved ability to manage yourself and your situation, to take control at appropriate times, is a major asset. But control, in this sense, means being able to start things, as well as stop them.

Just make a change and you take control

Thomas Edison, inventor of the electric light bulb, the gramophone and a thousand other useful devices, used to deal with his mental blocks and get the ideas flowing by shutting himself away for hours in the dark of the cupboard under the stairs. Lesser mortals, a century or so later, fiddle with some of the more garish screen colour schemes available on their PCs to jolt themselves awake and give themselves a break from the prosaic tyranny of the usual light grey and blue screen. The underlying idea, that you introduce something different or change your environment to change your relationship with it and destabilise your own unproductive state, goes back beyond the beginnings of NLP and beyond Edison, too. It is something people have been doing for hundreds of years. Yet it is also something that generations and individuals seem to have to rediscover again for themselves.

Making a change, in order to retake control of some aspects of your situation, is one of the most powerful basic techniques for managing yourself and managing your life. If you take action to change the state you are in, which is something that is largely under your own control, it immediately changes the way you feel about things and reminds you that you are in charge of your life. Depending on the circumstances, you will usually have many options about what to change. Let's get really specific. What could you actually do right now to change your state?

Three ways to change your state

1. Engage your body – skip to a more resourceful state.

Change how you're functioning physiologically and you'll feel different. There are a thousand ways you could do this, but here is one you probably haven't thought of. Buy yourself a skipping rope. When you need to change your state, skip for one minute. When that gets too easy, make it two minutes. You don't have to be stuck with that familiar low-energy feeling, when it's so easy

to do something about it. Skipping is effective because it is good
aerobic exercise that raises your metabolic rate and increases the
amount of oxygen in your system. Within a minute or two, you
will have moved yourself into a more positive state, mentally and
physically, and done no harm to your overall fitness, either.

2. Engage your mind – go and tidy up.

Start thinking differently and you'll change your state. Find some
manageable area, such as your desk, or a chest of drawers, and
spend a few minutes bringing order out of chaos. This can be a
very satisfying and fulfilling process. It eases you into decision-
making mode, nourishes your sense of competence and gives a
great feeling of getting down to business.

3. Engage with others – reconnect with someone.

Change how you feel in relation to others and you'll change your
state. Phone, e-mail or write to someone you value whom you
have not contacted for too long. If you have access to e-mail, this
can be ideal, because it allows you to remake the connection,
quickly and emphatically. Or maybe you'd prefer to make that
surprise call. Since people's sense of connectedness is so important, re-establishing a link with someone in this way is a positive,
constructive action that will almost always leave you feeling
better in yourself.

These three routes to changing your state – engaging your body,
engaging your mind and engaging with others – make it clear
that there is always something you can do to reassert an element
of personal control in your immediate environment. When you
do this, you are taking the initiative, albeit sometimes on a very
small scale, and, with it, taking on some element of responsibility for your feelings and responses.

This is another of the key points about self-management and life management. If you want to make the most of yourself and your life, it is essential to make sure you treat your life and your feelings as if they are truly your own. That implies, for example, that much of what goes on around you will be initiated or influenced by you, and that, far more often than people are always happy to accept, you can have some effect on much of what happens to you.

We are not saying that accidents and illness are your own fault; still less that they represent some kind of judgement upon you. We are saying that the tendency many people have to blame others for everything they feel unhappy about is a debilitating and corrosive habit – and one that can wreck people's lives, with no help from any outside agencies. Like so many of the ways people manage to limit and undervalue themselves, it involves accepting a view of life that is often passed down from parents, inculcated by teachers or bosses at an impressionable age, or made to seem inevitable by the constant drip-feed of attitudes from the people you are with from day to day, at work and at home.

If there is one thing we can promise you'll gain from this book, it's a clear understanding of just how much such second-hand attitudes can hold you back and just how easy it is to wave them goodbye, once you have the confidence to do so. You can do it. We can show you how.

In the course of the next few chapters, we'll be showing you a range of simple, tried and tested tools that can help you release more of your personal and professional potential than you ever thought possible. We will introduce you to your own Secret CV – the career résumé that looks forward to what you could do, rather than back to what you have done – and show you how to compile a ten-day Diary of Delights, a simple tool that can transform the way you look at the world. When it comes to it, though, you are the only one who can take the initiatives that will make you happier, healthier and richer. We can only describe and explain the techniques and point out some of the insights we've gained from working with companies, large and small, and teaching NLP to thousands of individual people, of all ages and many nationalities. There's no doubt though, that the development of NLP has made it easier than ever to put yourself squarely in control of your life. There has never been such a practical set of tools to help you be who you are and get what you want. If you're ready to manage yourself, manage your life and manage your relationships, you'll find that here is a very good place to start.

Chapter 2

Putting Yourself in the Driving Seat

Those see nothing but faults that seek for nothing else.
Thomas Fuller MD

Blame is a dangerous game

When Cindy comes home from school complaining that the teachers don't know their subjects, the exams are unfair, everyone's got it in for her and David, her boyfriend, has refused to speak to her, it is not going to be difficult to work out which of these statements is most likely to be strictly and literally true. There are poor teachers. Test papers are occasionally angled towards parts of the syllabus that have not been adequately taught. And it is not unknown for the entire population of a school to turn against one person, if that person has really been going out of his or her way to court unpopularity. But how likely are all these things? Isn't it much more likely that Cindy's black mood is simply triggered by item number four on her list of complaints? David's not speaking to her, and a community of several hundred children and adults is being held responsible for the fact that she's feeling bad.

Schooldays are a time for learning and hopefully Cindy will have moved on from this way of reacting to the world within the next few years. But there are still plenty of adults who have never quite left this sort of thinking behind. Whenever boom turns to bust, the financial pages are crowded with directors of substantial public companies trying to find scapegoats to blame for cyclical downturns in their markets. Often the downturns are, to all intents and purposes, acts of God, or at least the working out of worldwide economic and geopolitical trends that no one manager or board of directors could hope to buck. Even more often, the blamers and scapegoat-seekers bear partial responsibility themselves for their companies' failure to take evasive action when caught in the downdraught.

The self-serving nature of the blame game is seen at many different levels, as boards blame individuals, institutional investors blame boards, and governments and pundits wade in to blame the institutions for their 'short-termism'. This is a macho culture in which no one dares to come out with his hands up and admit that there are some forces you just can't fight. If you happen to be in the wrong place at the wrong time, no amount of management skill and business acumen is necessarily going to make things right.

Blaming people after the event doesn't make it unhappen. Worse, it keeps people's minds focused on the unalterable failures of the past, when they could much more profitably be looking forward to the opportunities of the future.

Cindy's blaming everyone else helps reinforce her belief that she is a victim and that she has no responsibility for her own experience of life. But it doesn't help her get what she wants. In the same way, all the corporate scapegoating and bloodletting that goes on does not usually help companies do anything positive to improve their ability to cope.

From problem frame to outcome frame

If you habitually focus your attention on something, you tend to get more of it in your life. If you look for problems, you'll find plenty of them. If you spend a lot of your time in contemplation of your own failures, you will always have plenty to occupy your thoughts. Fixating on who is to blame for some past disaster is rarely particularly useful. There may be lessons to be learned by analysing what happened and what the causes were, though the way history stubbornly refuses to repeat itself exactly often makes such learning distinctly suspect. But just knowing who you can pin the blame on is seldom any use at all.

When approaching similar situations in future it would be more useful to find a way of handling them that was more resourceful, flexible and inventive. What would it be like, for example, if you could avoid being hypnotised by problems? Instead of asking 'What's the problem?' and then trying to solve it, you would change gear and engage a way of thinking that might well lead you to a different set of answers. Instead of 'What's wrong?', you could start from a different point by asking 'What is it I really want?'

This approach introduces more options and automatically moves you towards a more flexible attitude. The first question frames the situation as a problem; the second is already looking forward, towards the idea of a positive outcome. To most people, the distinction between the two might seem pretty insignificant.

But it is actually quite fundamental, because it makes a world of difference to the kind of answers that emerge.

The question of how an issue is framed is a subject that has been pursued very energetically in NLP, over more than twenty years. The word 'frame' is just a metaphor, of course, but it is one that has proved to have many useful applications in down-to-earth, practical contexts. The idea is that you are able to choose the frame you adopt when you picture a situation, and then change the frame, quite deliberately, when you want to look at it again in a different light. As happens with a painting, the frame plays a significant part in determining how you see what is in front of you. But in this case the frame is imaginary – and therefore entirely under your conscious control. You may not have any control over the content of the picture, but you have plenty of control over how you choose to frame it.

This technique of thinking in terms of an outcome frame, rather than a problem frame, is a practical, robust tool you can use to lever yourself out of the rut of problem-centred thinking. Try it out and you will quickly be able to get a glimpse of its surprising potential. To see for yourself, take a pen and paper and note down, now, a real issue, at home or at work, that is of some importance to you. Then focus on that issue and apply these two sets of questions to it, noticing what very different responses the questions trigger. Do one, then the other.

Problem frame
What is my problem?
How long have I had it?
Where does the fault lie?
Who is to blame?
What is my worst experience with this problem?
Why haven't I solved it yet?

Outcome frame
What do I want?
How will I know when I've got it?
What else will improve when I get it?
What resources do I have already that can help me achieve this outcome?
What is something similar that I have succeeded in doing?
What is the next step?

The answers to the problem frame questions may explain some aspects of the situation, but they also serve to direct the focus of your attention straight back towards the past. Though these questions may help to clarify what has been going on, you can often end up feeling thoroughly tired and demotivated when taking this well-worn route. On the other hand, when you use the outcome frame questions in the right-hand column, the difference can be quite startling. For many people, it's a revelation to approach the situation in this way. The whole process feels more interesting and far more likely to trigger bold or offbeat thinking and new ideas you can turn to practical use.

Reframing as a practical tool

These different questions can be used for personal and professional issues. They are very effective for any individual wanting to get clear about where they're at and where they're going. Equally they can also be used to manage, lead and focus a team's thinking.

Let's take the example of a company that is trying, so far unsuccessfully, to launch a new product. Running down the list of 'problem frame' questions only produces the usual answers. The launch campaign was put back and lacked impact, the production and marketing departments are busy blaming each other and the reasons offered in answer to the last question

('Why haven't we solved it yet?') range from poor product design and bad media buying to uncompetitive pricing and stubbornly conservative customers. People's simple survival needs – and specifically the requirement to keep a job – make it hard, in this kind of culture, for anyone to admit that he or she may be responsible for things going wrong.

Now look at what happens, in the same circumstances, when a similar group of people decides to take the 'outcome frame' approach. 'What do we want?' helps to clarify the position. ('OK, we'd like to achieve full national distribution, but we'd settle for, perhaps, the South and South-east.') 'How will we know when we've got it?' might produce an answer based on, say, getting the product into 40 per cent of the potential outlets and achieving 11 per cent market share. 'What else will improve when I get it?' leads to the recognition that other lines would certainly be boosted by a successful sell-in of the new product, making it easier, for example, to justify an increase in the campaign budget.

When the discussion moves on to 'What resources do I already have that can help me?', the momentum really starts to pick up. Marketing and sales people may begin to realise that their existing contacts in the South mean that a relaunch focused on this part of the country would be far more likely to achieve success, while design and production specialists begin to think in terms of using common components and sub-assemblies, shared with other products, to cut costs and simplify manufacturing processes. And when it comes to 'What is something similar that I have succeeded in doing?', instead of referring back to the failures of a few weeks ago, people are encouraged to think about what they did right the last time they had a launch that really worked well. Out of all this, the answers to the last question ('What is the next step?') will often emerge with surprising clarity and certainty. Instead of a demoralising post-mortem, using the outcome frame approach can make such a meeting a starting point for a new and positive effort.

Business people we have trained to use this technique are invariably delighted to see how much difference it can make. There are sceptics in almost every training group and they are usually the ones who are most surprised at what reframing can do. Even if they have just gone through the motions, reading off the questions and applying them, one at a time, to the issue in hand, they are often taken aback by their own successes. They say things like 'I suppose I hadn't realised some of these alternatives were possible', and they are often surprised to find that they end the session with a clear sense of what needs to be done next.

But, of course, there is no magic about all this. It works because it is grounded in some very basic aspects of people's psychology. Each of the outcome frame questions naturally directs your thinking towards the future and towards the opportunities you have for exercising choice, inventiveness and imagination – and how you decide to frame your experience and the issues facing you will always have a huge influence on your response. Pick an issue you have and use these two sets of questions to give yourself some new choices.

In practice, much of the art of personal resource management comes down to just this – a simple matter of picking the right frame, so that you are helped rather than hindered in your thinking about what to do next. As you become better at moving yourself into fresh perspectives by changing the frame you use, you will be able to draw on much more of your own ingenuity and creativity in managing the situations around you.

Tomorrow's hindsight today – the 'as-if' frame

Another simple way of engineering this kind of perspective shift in yourself and other people is to employ the NLP reframing technique called the 'as-if' frame. This can have almost magical effects, in terms of loosening up and liberating people's thinking, because of the way it engages their creative potential. It seems, at first sight, like a very modest tool, but it can be extraordinarily powerful.

Whenever you go through the process of imagining a scenario and trying it on, as if it were real, you are making use of this technique. One particular way to exploit it is to go into the future and look back from there, as if the things you are thinking about had already happened. When faced with a tangle of options, or a difficulty that needs to be solved or sidestepped, you can use the as-if approach to force a shift of perspective. There are two steps to the technique:

1.   Jump ahead, in your mind, to a specific point well beyond your immediate uncertainties.
2.   Look back on the problems as if they had already been safely and successfully overcome.

Patrick really wasn't sure whether or not he wanted to have children. His partner, Jenny, knew that was what she wanted. He was troubled because he really loved her and he knew he wanted to be with her, but it seemed such a big – and long – commitment. Using the as-if frame he imagined how life would be, not just next year, or even when the children became teenagers. He went thirty years forward and imagined how it would be if he'd solved the problem back then by never having had them. In Patrick's words, 'I got a real shock. Without them it was so empty and I knew I'd missed one of the best bits of my life. It was so clear.' Patrick is now the father of two boys.

In a business context, pick an arbitrary date, say, one year ahead, and look back on the situation from that viewpoint. Ask yourself 'What did we have to do to get from there to here?' or 'What was it that made it possible for us to succeed like this?' In other words, assume for the moment that the success has happened and examine it retrospectively.

We all know everything looks simpler and clearer with the benefit of hindsight. Here is your chance to make this work in your favour. Instead of peering forward into a future that always looks fuzzy and divergent, full of branching alternatives and possibilities that depend on sequences of events that may or may not happen, you can clear away vast swathes of clutter. Looking forward is dauntingly open-ended. Looking back, everything seems more linear, more logical and inevitable, as if things could only ever have panned out one way.

When you operate within the as-if frame, you are using your imagination to experience a future that has turned out in a desirable way. In practice, though, this future, like everything else, will arise as a consequence of various earlier causes and events. The as-if perspective lets you glimpse a completely different angle on what has to have happened to make the future you want come true.

If it's good enough for Einstein ...

There's an idea we can borrow here from Albert Einstein, who always claimed he was no good at thinking in abstractions and therefore developed the idea of doing what he called 'thought experiments', so that he could just 'watch' what would happen if his theories about relativity were put into effect. Try a thought experiment in which you imagine you are looking back from a position twelve months from now in which your company's sales have risen by, say, 40 per cent. Use the as-if frame. Examine the situation as if this dramatic success was established fact. If you do this, it will be instantly obvious that radical changes must have occurred in some aspects of your business. You didn't get that 40 per cent sales growth just by doing exactly what you were doing before.

To register a gain of 40 per cent, you must have done something very substantial to alter your product or service, or the way it was perceived by the customer, or the way you sold it. Perhaps you upgraded what you offer to provide some advantage customers could not get anywhere else. Perhaps you broke ranks and took a bold pricing initiative that redefined your market and left your competitors gasping. Perhaps you moved from selling regionally through a traditional field salesforce to selling globally, twenty-four hours a day, via your new Web site. Whatever the change was, it cannot have been a matter of tinkering around the edges or it wouldn't have produced the new situation. Try out all the different change factors you can think of in your thought experiment and see which one seems to fit with the observed sales growth of 40 per cent. We're all of us a lot cleverer than we often give ourselves credit for, in matters like this, and it is highly likely that you will be able to gather useful information from this experiment.

Now try another thought experiment, in a personal context, again based on the as-if theme. Go forward another year. Imagine you have achieved real personal happiness, on a scale that you never thought possible. What does that feel like? What is different for you about feeling this way? So what is it that you did to bring about this change? If the result is so special, you can be sure that what you did won't just be whatever you were used to doing in the past. One of the strengths of the as-if frame is the way it always tends to turn you back towards the central truth that it's up to you to make things change for the better. That is why managing yourself always has to come first, before managing your life.

The perfect tool for picking deadlocks

For all its simplicity, the as-if frame is a genuinely powerful tool for thinking. It is also a good example of an NLP technique you can bring into play without anyone else noticing that anything particularly unusual is going on. For instance, there is nothing at all strange about intervening to break the stalemate in a bogged-down business meeting by using such an unobtrusive mechanism. If the discussion is going nowhere, try asking a question that will set up an as-if frame for everyone in the room.

> *'When we look back on how we dealt with this in two years' time, what do we think the important points will have been?'*

Asking a question like this is not going to upset anyone's expectations or lay you open to charges of being manipulative. It appears to work on a completely straightforward and mundane level. But it will, nevertheless, steer people round towards viewing the *impasse* from a more productive angle and serve to help them avoid being mesmerised by the difficulties ahead.

Like all the best techniques, the as-if frame is just as useful away from work. If you are going to go for what you want in life and avoid drift and inertia, you don't necessarily want some grand, over-detailed master plan. But you will, almost certainly, find yourself doing more planning and thinking ahead than you have usually done in the past, if only to ensure that the progress you make does move you towards what you really want.

It's easy to be sidetracked. It's easy to pick up other people's ideas and objectives, like their flu germs, just by being around them. The world is full of well-meaning people who always think they know better than you what you want and what you should be doing with your life. And since it is often easier to persuade an individual not to do something than to inspire him or her to act, most of these advisers spend a lot of their time telling you what you can't do and why you can't do it.

This is the sort of situation where the as-if frame really comes into its own. As a way of testing, quickly, whether the good reasons that have been advanced for not doing something are quite as sound as they seem, there is nothing like jumping ahead a few pages in the script and grabbing a quick glimpse of what might really happen.

Fast-forward to explore your future

When Kim and Simon started thinking about buying a home together, after a year of living in rented accommodation, they received a great deal of conflicting advice about what to look for, where to look and how much to spend. Though they were convinced the relationship would last, the degree of commitment involved in owning property together seemed daunting for a young couple. Yet, on the other hand, the cost of buying would be only a little more each month than the rent they were already paying. With the help of a friend who had taken an NLP practitioner training course, Kim used the as-if frame technique to gain a new perspective on her situation and find out more about what she really wanted.

She decided to fast-forward three years, to her twenty-fifth birthday, and take a look back from that viewpoint. To her surprise, she was able to imagine herself quite clearly in this future situation, in a house full of her's and Simon's things. The sense of ownership was very strong, and she realised that this was something that really made a difference. From this perspective, it suddenly struck her that the house was not so much a place for living in, or an investment, as a key part of the future she and Simon would create for themselves and the lifestyle they would choose. For example, though it hadn't seemed to matter much before, she now saw that a garden would be important – having a space of their own, out in the open air, where they could sit and talk and laugh with their friends. A house, she realised, would only work for them if it helped them enjoy their lives together.

Back in the present, the process of househunting was transformed by this. Finding the right property became a matter of finding the house that fitted this future, rather than the one that looked best on paper or offered the largest rooms for the money. It wasn't going to be the estate agent's details or a surveyor's report that told her what to buy. Whenever they went to view a house now, Kim could tell in a couple of minutes whether it was right or not, because she had a clear feeling about how it was supposed to be. When the right place came along, with a tiny patio garden and a neglected interior, she knew at once that it had the potential to be the home they wanted. Simon backed her judgement and they ended up living there for several years before moving onwards and upwards.

The insight Kim acquired through using the as-if frame enabled her to know what she really wanted and manage this area of her life better. By being clearer about what she needed, she was able to sift the possible options put forward by estate agents and make a choice that helped to move her towards it. By choosing, Kim was already starting to shape the future she wanted and make it begin to come true.

This is NLP at work in a very practical way. Some people are much better than others at knowing whether a house will work for them – and it is not all down to coincidence. Through being shown how to apply the as-if methodology, Kim had learnt a new skill that enabled her to move forward with more confidence, knowing what she was moving towards. And, as she quickly realised, its applications went far beyond househunting.

Hurdling nearby difficulties and using the as-if frame to see what the situation looks like from the other side is such a quick and handy technique that you could soon be doing it automatically, without even thinking. Like many of the other ideas in this book, it will soon become a part of the way you habitually approach decisions and problems – a way of keeping your mind and your options open to maximise your chances of success in whatever you do.

By assembling your own toolkit of practical techniques to help you see new perspectives and fresh possibilities, you can help yourself move towards a richer and more satisfying future, in both your work and your personal relationships. You can develop and refine the essential skills that are needed to manage your life more effectively than ever before – and move on out from that to manage your interaction with other people. All true management begins with self-management. And all true self-management, inevitably, begins with self-knowledge.

'As simple as possible ... but not simpler'

In the next few chapters, we will be drawing on our own experience, the expertise developed within the loose-knit worldwide community of NLP and insights from a multitude of other sources to help you find out a little more about yourself and a lot more about your potential.

Einstein once said that he believed human beings used no more than one-tenth of their brainpower. He also said: 'Everything should be made as simple as possible ... but not simpler.' There are a lot of major issues to do with how we live our lives that have become unnecessarily complex and convoluted in recent years. One of the main aims of this book is to help you cut through all this and develop strategies for simplifying what can safely be made simple, without pretending there's an easy answer to everything.

A key part of the art of managing is noticing what works and recognising just what will give you the most leverage. Though you are only at the end of Chapter 2 of this book, you have already been introduced to a range of important techniques that you can use straight away to make a real difference in many home and work situations. But have you noticed – and have you tried them out? By way of review here's a checklist:

1. **Pleasure spot-checks** (p. 13)
   Learn to pay attention to what is enjoyable and have more of it.

2. **Associating and dissociating** (pp. 14–15)
   Know when and how to increase the feeling and when to step back to see things dispassionately.

3. **Three ways to change your state** (pp. 16–17)
   Engage your body, engage your mind, engage with others – whichever you do you'll change how you're feeling and that means you'll have new choices available to you.

4. **Outcome frame** (pp. 23–4)
   Stop blocking yourself with problem thinking. Start from what you want and go forward from there.

5. **As-if frame** (pp. 26–8)
   Think as if a change you seek has already occurred, in order to get clear about just how you achieved it. Or, if you're not sure you want a change, check out how your

life will be further down the line if you don't do anything now.

The point is that some of the most powerful self-management tools are very quick and easy to learn. If you tend to believe that change is necessarily difficult and you are expecting to encounter complicated and demanding techniques that take a long time to master, you may be surprised. Keep reading and you could find yourself picking up a range of tools that will help you get what you want in no time at all.

Chapter 3

What Do You Want?

The desire of the end will point out the means.
William Hazlitt

Life's key skill

The ability to know what you want is the single most important skill in managing both yourself and your life. It is the
single factor that enables you to set a course and know where you
are heading, and why you are going there.

If there is one key skill we should be teaching our children,
this is it. But many of us are so bad at knowing what we want
ourselves that we'd have virtually nothing useful to teach a
younger generation. Even in business, the rudimentary goal-
setting skills that are taught in conventional MBA courses are
less than satisfactory. If NLP had nothing else to offer the world,
the fact that it has developed clear, systematic and practical ways
of helping people work towards finding out what they really
want would be enough to make both business and individuals sit
up and take notice.

There is no question you can ask yourself that is more vitally important than this. It is all to do with the way the mind works, or the technology of the imagination. It is best demonstrated by looking at the arts. How does a film-maker, a novelist, a painter, a poet or a photographer engage our imagination? Each of them does it by being specific, by selecting details with particular power and resonance, and investing them with emblematic significance. A child's glove in the snow may mean nothing at all. A long, slow pan across a snow-covered park, eventually lighting on a red glove and then tracking back until it is just a speck in the distance, becomes a poignant emotional moment in the language of the cinema. The phrase 'a host of golden daffodils' can make words on paper trigger a genuine visual experience, despite the fact that daffodils are usually any shade of yellow but gold.

Being specific is one of the most potent ways we have of making an experience vivid, whether it is a picture, a sensation, a sound, a taste or smell. Try to imagine biting into a raw fruit. Now try again, bearing in mind the new and specific knowledge that the fruit is a gooseberry. That makes quite a difference, doesn't it? If you listen to the people who seem to be the most engaging and generate the most interest and enthusiasm when they talk, you notice that this is usually a direct result of their ability to make what they're saying come alive.

Their language is peppered with colourful phrases that help you recreate in your mind the scenes they describe, so that you can see them, feel involved in them and sometimes even hear, taste or smell what's going on. Charles Dickens was a master of this, picking out a profusion of odd and evocative details to bring each scene of stories like *Oliver Twist* and *Great Expectations* vividly to life.

If someone who is trying to communicate with you gives you nothing but generalities and nothing to catch your imagination, you just glaze over and lose interest, however hard you are trying to concentrate – as anyone who has sat through a conference while speaker after speaker drones on in a welter of well-meaning abstractions knows. Indeed, trying to force yourself to concentrate on something so featureless and hard to pin down produces its own hypnotic trance.

When other people do it to you, it's obvious – you very quickly get bored and lose concentration when you are presented with an unstimulating, non-specific experience. But if it's boring when other people do it, in the external world, it is mind-numbingly tedious when you do it to yourself, on the inside.

A pull like the force of gravity

How you represent reality, memories and imagined situations to yourself is a matter of huge importance. It is crucial in determining how interested and excited you can be about your dreams and your goals, how vivid and compelling you can make them and therefore how motivated you will be towards achieving them. If you are boring yourself when you think or dream about your future, it will not engage your enthusiasm and draw you towards it.

If you have no specific idea of the future you want, you will not even be able to know, day by day, if you are moving in the right direction or not. Do you want happiness and fulfilment? How are you going to judge whether something you do is going to move you nearer those goals or take you off somewhere else, at a tangent? How are you even going to be sure you'd recognise it if you suddenly achieved happiness? If you were happy, what would that be like, specifically? What would an outsider observe that would confirm you had attained happiness? Never mind an outsider, what would you see, hear and feel that would make it clear *to you* that you had found the happiness you were seeking?

It is only when you get down to this level of specific definition that your idea of happiness starts to differentiate itself from other people's generalised notions. Until your personal idea of happiness is defined in terms of what really has value for you, it's just so much public property, without the power to move and motivate you. Give it the time and attention to develop into your own highly individual creation and it will pull you towards it with a force as predictable and unwavering as gravity.

How to set goals that work for you

People do better, in business and life, if they know what they are trying to achieve and why. A positive, attractive goal begins immediately to create the preconditions for its own fulfilment. Indeed, one of the reasons so few people appear to get the satisfaction they desire from life is simply that so few take the trouble to decide what they are prepared to commit themselves to as really important personal goals.

The essential rules of goal-setting are simple, though the skills and principles involved are rarely understood. The basics can be summed up in three sentences:

1. Your goal must be **POSITIVE** and stated in overtly positive terms.
2. Your goal must be **SPECIFIC** and capable of being written down.
3. Your goal must be **VERIFIABLE**.

The insistence that your goal must be formulated in positive terms is a very important discipline. 'I don't want to smoke any more' is the classic example of a negatively phrased goal. Because it is impossible to imagine not smoking, except by referring back to the idea of smoking, this would guarantee that the would-be non-smoker's attention was focused back on to cigarettes every time his or her goal was considered. You can do – and imagine doing – positive things. You simply cannot envisage *not* doing something, without thinking of that very thing first and then, somehow, trying to negate it and drive it from your mind. The parent who calls 'Mind you don't fall down' to the child climbing up the slide is actually increasing the chance of the infant falling. All proposed goals that contain words like 'not' and 'no' need to be turned round to focus on the positive change they are really about.

But there are subtler forms of negative goals that are equally pernicious. 'I want to give up smoking' is another almost useless goal, because it is clearly about being deprived of something that the goal-setter does not wholeheartedly want to let go of. Every time the well-intentioned smoker contemplated that goal, he or she would be firmly reminded of the fact that breaking free from the addiction of smoking was seen as a deprivation. 'I want to cut down on the number of customer complaints we receive' is another false positive in the same class. There is no 'not' in sight, but it still urgently needs to be re-cast, preferably into some constructive form such as 'I want our service to amaze our customers, so that they will happily pay a premium to deal with us'. This is not just smoke and mirrors. It really makes a fundamental difference when goals are rephrased in ambitious and positive terms.

Almost anything that you are tempted to say in a negative way can be reshaped like this. And it is well worth making the effort, because it will have a real impact on the results you get. Suppose, however, that when you ask yourself what you want, all you can come up with is a negative formulation, such as 'to stop working so hard'. Though it is phrased negatively, that doesn't mean it's a bad plan. It merely needs to be worked on a little more. Just press ahead and take it a stage further. 'OK, so I don't want to work so hard. That's what I *don't* want. And if I wasn't working so hard, what would that do for me?'

The answer might be, for example, 'Well, then I'd be able to spend more time with my family.'

'*So what do you want?*'
'I want to spend more time with my family.'

Now you have an answer you can work with – one that is stated in the positive. This is a goal that takes you to the core of the change you are trying to make and will draw you on towards its realisation.

How will you know?

Now that the goal you are refining is a positive one, stated in positive terms, you are ready to subject it to the next test, to see if it is verifiable. Again, there is a key question that will establish this once and for all:

'*How will you know when you've got it?*'

For some people, the success that counts shows on the outside, with recognition, money or acceptance into a particular social or professional group. For others, the symbols of success couldn't be more different. What these people need may be much more personal and internalised – approval from parents, admiration from their children or even an inner sense of achievement with no obvious external signs. Asking 'How will you know when you've got it?' can trigger an exploration of the criteria that motivate you and the symbols that represent those criteria.

Whether for yourself or with others, you should push for specifics by pressing this point home and asking:

'What will you see, hear and feel that will let you know you have achieved what you were aiming for?'

You are trying to establish what specific sensory signals will demonstrate, beyond doubt, that you have succeeded in reaching your goal. When you can define the evidence that will prove to you that your goal has been attained, you will be able to focus, clearly and unambiguously, on what you want. This clarity gives you a sense of purpose and direction that starts to pay off almost immediately – long before you are even close to achieving your desired outcome. People with a clear outcome in their heads stop feeling sorry for themselves and casting themselves as victims of circumstance. Their ambitions acquire shape and dignity and their subconscious processes are automatically tuned in and set to work on the task of making the link between the present situation and the future goals. The more you focus in on the outcome you want and the more time you spend thinking about it, the more you will move towards making the thousand little adjustments in your life and work that will inch you along, day by day, in the right direction.

The idea that the goals or desired outcomes you focus on should be clear and specific ('What do you want?'), stated in the positive and verifiable through direct evidence from the senses ('How will you know when you've got it? What will you see, hear and feel?') is an important part of NLP's refinement of the art of goal-setting. By insisting that goals must be clear, positive and open to sensory proof, NLP guides people towards the creation of 'well-formed outcomes' – outcomes which, because of their clarity and coherence, will always stand a better chance of becoming reality than less rigorously defined objectives.

Any time, any place, anywhere?

There are at least two more handy 'well-formedness conditions' that you can use to add muscle to your goals. The first involves asking yourself whether you literally want what you want all the time and everywhere you go:

'In what context do I want this?'

In other words, when, where and with whom? As a continuous presence or only in the context of one part of your life? The sensual tenderness and playfulness that are appropriate to your most intimate moments might, for example, be distracting in the context of a tough, no-holds-barred business negotiation. To want but not to think about the context is to risk becoming a modern King Midas.

The other useful, and often highly significant, question to measure your desired outcome against is:

'What are the pay-offs to me from the present situation?'

The way things are at present may be unsatisfactory in some respects, but it may also be giving you some unacknowledged pay-offs. Your conscious mind may know perfectly well that change is needed. But if you are subconsciously deriving unrecognised benefits from the present situation, the risk of innocent and ingenious self-sabotage is very high.

Many smokers find their sensible decisions about giving up cigarettes are compromised by a range of positive by-products – having something to do with your hands in social situations, having a reward system you can activate to cheer yourself up or, for adolescents, feeling grown-up and rebellious with a cigarette in your mouth. Set against the heightened risks of emphysema, lung cancer and so on, these should not be decisive factors. In the real world, they often are. Until you identify and acknowledge the positive by-products that could be lost when change occurs, you are not looking at the full reality of the situation.

If you have tried to give up smoking before, but taken it up again, this is feedback in itself. If you want to be more successful in future, you're going to have to do something different. Instead of fighting yourself, why not try taking yourself seriously and assuming, for the moment, that you have very good reasons for smoking? Make your own list, coming back to it over a couple of days. Be curious. Even if your reasons seem strange, do not censor your list. When you have compiled a full list, look at it and think about how you are going to be able to get all these benefits in some other way. Stop making the change a struggle. Don't cut yourself off from the benefits. Just find new ways of taking them with you and getting these pay-offs. If, for instance, you enjoy the camaraderie of standing outside the office with the other smokers, find an alternative way to get those feelings of sociability and togetherness.

In workshops, we have sometimes deliberately taken the time to tease out all the pay-offs from an unwanted behaviour – the record, for smoking, is thirty-two reasons. And this kind of ambivalence applies not only to individuals. We have seen companies, too, completely stuck and unable to move forward because of their inability or reluctance to recognise that they are unlikely to change as long as people are so heavily invested in current practices. The less aware people are of the pay-offs the greater the shock, sense of loss or trauma that may accompany enforced change.

For some years after the introduction of fibre optic cables and digital telephone switching, British Telecom, which then employed nearly a quarter of a million people, failed to adapt to the new situation. The new technology meant the company needed to be, at most, half its previous size. But most people at

BT were one-company employees, lifers who had never worked anywhere else, and if there was to be a 50 per cent payroll cull, everyone in the organisation would have to watch many, many friends and colleagues lose their jobs. The pay-off from the situation as it stood was that everyone's friends stayed in comfortable employment. While no one rocked the boat and BT's efficiency measures slipped further and further behind its international competitors, there were no big cutbacks. But when top management finally decided to bite the bullet, 100,000 people were paid off. Wave after wave of redundancies eventually brought the headcount down and efficiency levels up, at a cost of several hundred million pounds in severance payments, and BT discovered a new ability to compete in the marketplace.

For both individuals and businesses, it is vital to identify all the significant by-products of the current situation before trying to implement change. Once you know what these pay-offs are, you can devise the ways you need to keep them and take them with you when you go.

Cranking the handle

Before we leave the subject of outcomes and goals, there is one more simple, two-part goal exploration and setting technique that you should know about. At first sight, it seems almost too simple, but we have seen it work successfully for literally thousands of people. And there is virtue in its very simplicity. As one corporate manager said: 'As a technique, there's nothing to it. It's so easy. It's just like cranking a handle. But what comes out at the other end can really set you thinking.'

Until you have practised a few times, it is probably best to do this technique with the help of a friend or colleague, if only because the presence of another person forces you to crystallise thoughts into words. But there is no real reason why you should not try it on your own.

You have already had a glimpse of this approach at work, earlier in the chapter, when the question-and-follow-up sequence was used to trigger the insight that the person wanted to spend more time at home with the family. Taken all the way through, it is a much more powerful and versatile technique. The two parts of the process are two simple questions; the first, as always, being the fundamental question behind all goal-setting:

'*What do you want?*'

But it is the follow-up – and the looping technique that comes afterwards – that make this NLP technique especially effective:

'*What will that do for you?*'

You must resist the temptation to elaborate, reword or reinterpret either of the questions. Stick to the script. Allow time for the first answer to develop before moving on to the second and let the second answer go where it will, too. Then, again without changing the wording, loop back and ask the first question again:

'*So . . . what do you want?*'

Even if the immediate reaction is 'I've just told you', this is usually followed by a revised, clarified or expanded version of the first answer, which begins to carry the process of exploration forward.

There is quite a powerful intellectual and social prohibition against stubbornly repeating what you have just said, word for word. What's more, the answer to the 'What do you want?' question will automatically be framed, the second time around, in the light of the answer that has just been given to 'What will that do for you?'

It is well worth persevering and continuing this sequence, going round and round the loop, until you are sure you've got to what really matters. You can help this process by using an easy, wondering tone: you're not grilling the other person, you're exploring together. Notice, as the answers change and become more specific, how the questions themselves seem to fade into the background, until they are effectively just providing a prompt now and then to keep things moving along.

So what sort of useful information might you expect to glean from this process? At its best, it can trigger great and unexpected clarity about aims and priorities that might otherwise have remained obscure, because it helps people get clear about the ends they're going for versus the means they're employing to achieve them.

What's the end beyond the means?

Just asking 'What do I want?' is important, because it helps to ensure that you are running your own life, rather than leaving it to other people and their expectations to determine the shape it takes. Asking 'What would that do for me?' very often changes the level of the debate. The answer to the first question may be 'I want a new house/car/husband/sofa/baby'. The answer to the second is commonly pitched at a much more abstract level and will usually reveal something about what you truly value or need in your life. Thus, the house might bring security, the car status, the husband companionship, the sofa comfort and the baby unconditional love.

In the light of this, it is often obvious that the first outcome,

the answer to 'What do I want?' is only a means to an end. And
the end – whether it is security, status, companionship, comfort,
unconditional love or something else – is probably very important to you. You need to be able to spot the difference between
your means and your ends, if you are ever going to be able to
manage your life effectively.

When Darren was in his late teens, he developed an all-
consuming lust for big, old American cars. He was a big, tough
kid who found people difficult to get along with. And he wanted
his own Chevvy, with a passion that dwarfed family, job and
everything else in his life. He found his own ways of making
money to get the car of his dreams – and when they didn't
deliver the goods quickly enough, he started breaking into
people's houses and carried on until he was caught. He managed
to avoid prison, narrowly, and had been given a second chance
and a job in a warehouse when we were asked to talk to him.

There was hardly any point in asking Darren 'What do you
want?' The answer came back instantly. '*1956 Chevrolet*'.

'What would that do for you?'

A pause, then a gruff answer, '*I'd get respect.*'

'And if you got respect, what would that do for you?'

Long pause. '*I . . . I suppose I'd feel I belonged, like I was
someone, yeah?*'

Darren's vivid dream and urgent desire for the car was important all right, but clearly as a means to an end. His wish was for
the car, but his deeper desire was for respect and a proper sense
of identity.

If you were the manager who had been persuaded to give this

twenty-year-old criminal his last chance to get on the right track, would this kind of psychological information be of practical use to you in knowing how to handle him? The answer is that it would. It would be extremely useful to know that 'respect' however he defined it, was one of Darren's most highly valued criteria for feeling OK about himself.

This was privileged information, after all. Darren himself hadn't put his finger on what the desire to own such a car really meant for him, so he couldn't easily have said what he really wanted. As the manager in this situation said, you would hardly be going out to buy him the car to satisfy his need. But you could certainly look for justified opportunities to let him know that you respected him, and take very good care to see that other workers did not taunt him or pick on him for his awkward, ill-at-ease manner. The knowledge that respect was a key issue enabled his boss to manage him more effectively, making life easier for both Darren and the company. And, in the end, because he could prove a steady, reliable income, it became relatively easy for Darren to borrow the money he needed from the bank and buy himself a fine specimen of the car that had haunted his dreams.

It's in his kiss?

Once you have got used to it, there is nothing strange about the idea that one of the major tools for managing your life is simply asking what you want for yourself and what other people want to satisfy their needs. And since the answers that come back are so often couched in abstract terms, it makes a lot of sense to focus on the only reliable evidence we have to tell us whether our values are being honoured or violated – the behaviours we can observe.

A person may want to feel loved. But what convinces that person that all is well and that he or she actually is loved will usually be some specific action or behaviour that just happens to have become entrenched as a personal touchstone for love. People don't always realise this. They often fail to understand that all the conventional symbols of loving may leave someone completely cold, unless they are accompanied by one key behaviour that validates the rest. For some people it will be holding hands or eating a meal alone together. For others, it will be the way your partner always warns you to drive carefully, whenever you go out in the car, or the phone call in the middle of the day to see how your morning went. It is literally a case of 'whatever turns you on' – and you may have very little control over what does the trick for you. Whatever it is, though, what you are looking out for is the behaviour that means to you that you have what you want.

As your skill at exploiting the power of the 'What do you want?' technique grows, you will find that you can start the process at any level you choose and move smoothly up and down, from specifics to abstractions and back down to concrete details again. You can answer the basic question at the most materialistic level ('I want money', for example) and work up to explore what you imagine money will do for you and so be clear about what really matters to you at this time. You can start at the high abstract level ('I want commitment', for example) and work down to explore the specific behaviours that would prove to you, to your own satisfaction, that you've got the real thing.

Are you getting what you want?

At the beginning of this chapter, we said that the ability to know what you want was a key skill for life that everyone should develop and that should be made available to children as well. But part of the problem is that people are wary of introducing anything remotely systematic into their dealings with their inner selves or their dealings with others in their important relationships.

This is a strange, romantic notion, this belief that it is somehow better to bumble around feeling vulnerable and confused about what you want than to find ways of clarifying your goals and moving towards them. We just don't think that drift is beneficial in these matters. The techniques outlined in this chapter have had up to twenty-five years of use and development, and have helped to bring greater happiness, fulfilment and career success to many thousands of people. If you choose to practise and use them to the full, you can, if you want, make massive changes for the better in your life, starting here and now.

Chapter 4

Manage Yourself,
Manage Your Life

Every man is the architect of his own fortune.

Sallust

The hammer or the nail?

There are all sorts of reasons why you may have picked up a book about NLP and the practical art of managing your life. You may already be well on the way to achieving your life's goals – rich, healthy, loved, satisfied and fulfilled – but still realistic enough to believe that there could be something to be gained from other people's specialised knowledge and experience. On the other hand, you may be chugging along or feeling stuck in the doldrums or be piecing your confidence together again after disappointment or disaster. But wherever you are starting from, this book should go a long way towards ensuring that you feel ready to make the most of whatever comes next in your life.

In this chapter we will show you how to use simple, easily-learned NLP techniques which will enable you to make important changes in your life. We will show you how to:

1. Take charge of the state you are in and make the most of your personal resources.
2. Become more flexible, so that you always have more choice about what to do next.

We will introduce you to several new techniques that you can immediately begin to use and incorporate into your daily life and work. They will help you both manage your state – the physical, mental and emotional shape you are in at any particular time – and increase your flexibility, so that you can feel comfortable under pressure and perform well on demand. The more flexible you are, the more options you will have, whatever the situation. Learning what to do and how to do it in these two areas will bring you real benefits very quickly.

To live is to choose – to choose is to live

The secret of life is being able to choose how you live it. And to be able to choose, you need to really understand about the role of control. Not controlling other people, but where control lies in your own life. Does it lie out there, with others, or does it rest inside yourself? If you want to manage yourself and your life, it is vital that you pay attention to this question of where control is located. You cannot control the world, but you do control how you react to it. What you feel depends on the context, and it can flip into reverse at a moment's notice when a single element in that context changes slightly.

Imagine waiting in the rain, in a short, narrow, one-way street, for your partner to drive by and pick you up. As the drops trickle down the back of your neck, you probably think: 'I could really do with seeing that car come round the corner in the next ten seconds.' Then there's a squeal of tyres and another car swings round the bottom corner and starts tearing up the empty street the wrong way. Suddenly, you are standing in the rain hoping against hope that your partner has been held up and won't be along for another few minutes. The risk, even the outside chance, of a head-on meeting with a maniac instantly dwarfs all thoughts of discomfort and puts them into a bigger perspective. Your normal, sane reaction is to be willing to trade off any amount of standing in the wet in return for knowing there will be no crash. The rain is fine and your response to it is wholly changed by your perception of the new situation.

When you are really stressed and down in the dumps, such changes of perspective come slowly or not at all. There seems to be only one way to react to things, and it seems to be dictated by the world outside, so that you have no say in the matter and no element of choice. In the office environment, you frequently see people getting deep into this sort of quagmire. They find that they are constantly on the receiving end of other people's calls and queries on the phone. But before they can answer them, the phone is going again and someone has walked off with the papers they are looking for and a disk has appeared on the desk without any explanation of what's on it and they just want to scream 'Stop'. But they don't, usually. They stay late, trying to catch up, and discover that somehow getting back on level terms with the job seems to elude them, however many extra hours they put in.

If it feels as though life is causing things to happen to you and you're just doggedly treading water, something is wrong. If you feel as if you are never a cause, but always on the receiving end, then the 'locus of control' is in the wrong place. When you recognise that the locus of control – i.e. where control of the situation is located – is in the wrong place, it is time to take action to shift it from 'out there' to where it belongs, which is resting within you. If you put into action what follows in this book, you will achieve this and you will really start managing yourself and managing your life. And, fortunately, NLP offers some brilliantly simple and effective tools for doing this.

Take charge of the state you're in

Managing your life is not going to be just about getting rid of the things that don't work. It's going to be much more positive and proactive than that. It is going to be about reclaiming the initiative in your life now and shaping it for the future, to your own, individual, customised design and specification. That's not to say that you will end up with an inflexible blueprint – the unexpected will occur and you will need to have the flexibility to deal with it or welcome it as appropriate. It's more about having a clear sense of self, a sense of purpose and ultimately a sense, day by day, of a life well lived.

NLP provides some of the tools and techniques for making these high aspirations become reality, starting off, as demonstrated in the last chapter, with a lot of practical help towards finding your own answers to the crucial question 'What do I want?'. There could hardly be a more important question for any individual. And yet, many people, of all ages, are so intimidated by it that they cannot easily bring themselves to even begin working towards an answer.

Sometimes, just getting started is a large part of the problem. But often, there is also a fear of finishing, identifying your goal and then somehow letting yourself down and feeling bad because you've failed to achieve it. As one woman we worked with put it: 'If I don't get clear about what I really want, I'll never be too disappointed when I don't get it.'

And then there are people who fear that, by focusing on what they really want, they might be blind to other opportunities which come along afterwards. You spend ten years trying to reach a goal, only to discover, when you get there, that it wasn't really what you'd hoped for, or that you have long ago outgrown its attractions. For people who feel like this, it is important to understand that clarifying what you want is a continuing dynamic process. It is not something you do once and are then stuck with for the rest of your life. You are free to take stock and change your mind whenever you choose.

For that matter, it is quite OK not to know what you want. That knowledge is a perfectly legitimate starting point. For some people, finding out what they want from life *is* what they want – an end in itself, or perhaps the beginning of another journey. To know that you don't know and that you do want to know is a great deal better than conning yourself, distracting yourself and never facing the issue. It's not not knowing that's bad for you. It's abandoning yourself to the mercy of chance and other people's will and whims that leaves you feeling your life is not your own.

The NLP processes for teasing out and pinning down what you really want are very important indeed. But there are other NLP techniques that can have equally immediate practical applications. For example, you can get real help in taking charge of your own internal states. Imagine you are about to walk through a door, to enter an interview room, step out on to a stage for a presentation or a concert, or to go into an office for a tough, potentially confrontational negotiation. These are all situations where some people might feel a strong inclination to turn tail and bolt. You might have butterflies in your stomach or feel a rising tide of panic in your chest. Or you might feel keyed up, excited and anxious. You might even feel cool, relaxed and so dissociated from the whole situation that you are worried about appearing too casual and blasé to make the impact you want.

In any of these cases, what you may feel you need most is to be able to access a steady, resourceful state, in which you can perform at the very peak of your ability, with conviction, professionalism and power. It may, momentarily, seem rather unlikely. But if you know what to do, there are ways in which a few seconds' preparation can make all the difference to what happens when you step through that doorway.

Three steps to a resourceful state

To tap into the sort of state in which you can deliver your best, all you need to do is make use of a simple three-step technique, developed more than two decades ago, in the the early days of NLP, and since used successfully by thousands of people. It relies on the fact that, however tense or nervous you are, even if you can't directly change the way you feel you can change the way you think, and that then changes how you feel.

It is worth experimenting with this technique and practising it in situations that are not especially important to you, in order to be familiar with the sequence when you choose to do it for real, in situations where you really need it. The more you practise, the better you'll become – and the more surprised you'll be at the potency of this life-management tool.

Here is how to take control of your state using the three-step technique:

1. Get clear about what state you would ideally wish to be in.

You may need to be feeling bold and confident, sharp and imaginative, or warm, witty and engaging. Be as clear and specific as you can about what you are looking for and put it into words.

2. Recall a specific occasion in the past when you have been in that state.

What you are looking for here is not necessarily an exactly parallel situation. It's the feeling you had at that time that needs to be appropriate. Everyone has had days when they could do no wrong, when people seemed to be falling over themselves to help you and life just seemed to flow. Now just recall the time that's most appropriate for you right now.

3. Re-live it as vividly as you possibly can.

There's an art – and a little bit of science – to this. To make the recreation of your unstoppably positive state as vital and engrossing as possible, you need to immerse yourself as fully as you can in your memory of this specific occasion in the past. To do this, you will want to engage with as many aspects of the experience as you can. Instead of a vague, generalised memory, you need to recreate the specifics – the sights, the sounds, the external physical feelings and the internal sensations, the smells and even, perhaps, the tastes associated with that time.

The more specific sensory data you bring together to help you reconstitute the successful experience of the desired state in the past, the more powerfully it will act to influence your present state. As you re-live and reactivate the sensations of the confident, capable state, what is going on in your brain will start to trigger real, measurable physiological changes, affecting your pulse, your breathing, your muscle tone and posture, and even subtle factors like the dilation of your pupils and the conductivity of your skin.

You are changing what's going on in your brain, and that is changing your body and your internal state, so that you recapture your very best form, just when it is going to be of most use to you. You are not stepping off the edge into the unknown, remember. You have felt this good and this capable before. It's not as if you can't do it, because you are re-living, or even re-being, the way you have experienced being and feeling and acting in the past. This is a state that rightly belongs to you and your history. It's part of you, and all you are doing now is drawing on the bank of your experience to come up with what is appropriate for this particular day and this particular situation.

Whose state is it, anyway?

Yet, strangely enough, it is not your ownership of the experience that seems to matter. If you have never actually lived through the state that you believe is right for the situation you face, you may still find, as many people do, that you can use your imagination to tap into someone else's strengths and persona with remarkable effect. And the person who becomes your model for this exercise does not even have to have existed. Your chosen model can be a mythical or fictional character, just as readily as a real person, alive or dead.

The first stage of the resourcing process – achieving absolute clarity about what state you need to attain – is exactly the same as before. But once you have done that, you need to throw open your imagination to think what inspirational character has or had the power and the outlook you are in need of. The answer could be anybody, from Clint Eastwood to Dorothy Parker, from some member of your own family to Martin Luther King or from Galileo to Steffi Graf.

You don't even need to know a lot about him or her. You just need to feel sure the person you pick is a convincing embodiment, at least for you, of the qualities you need to 'borrow'. The same applies to a fictional figure, from a film, a book or TV, because you can then simply project the necessary qualities on to whichever character seems appropriate.

Once you have chosen your role model, step into the shoes of this person who embodies what you need and try the feeling on for size. Breathe as you imagine this person would breathe. If you have some privacy, go a little further. Stand the way your model would stand. Walk like he or she would walk. Try on a couple of typical facial expressions and the odd turn of phrase. Get inside the character and start to feel at home there. Explore the new perspective that comes with a new persona. Feel about your situation the way you imagine your model would feel. In less time than it takes to read this, you will have altered your mood and your state.

When you change your state, you change what feels possible for you and what you can accomplish. It's difficult to exaggerate how important this is. Managing your state is one of the keys to successfully managing yourself. Asking yourself what state would be useful and appropriate, given what you're seeking to accomplish, is a very different, genuinely empowering way of coming at life. It means you get to choose.

A different route to state control

Simple and effective as the three-steps method is as a way of managing your internal state, it is not the only technique NLP has developed for this important task. One alternative method, which can be used alone or with the help of an NLP practitioner or therapist, involves discovering what stands between you and the state that would be most appropriate for your situation. Again, the steps are simple:

1. Notice the state you are in now.

You want to feel calm, perhaps, but you actually feel angry. That's OK. You feel whatever you feel. But it is important to recognise and register this.

2. Ask yourself what it is that is preventing you from accessing the state you want.

The feeling of anger is stopping you from feeling calm, and it may well be that this anger is being triggered by what is happening around you now. Equally, however, it may not. It may be an example of the very common phenomenon of your past driving your present, which seldom does anyone any favours.

3. Focus on what you are feeling now and ride that feeling back into your past.

Reach back into your personal history and discover whether the experience of this emotion feels like something you remember feeling at an earlier time.

4. Find out if there is something in the past, which, if you let go of it, would allow you to feel what you want to feel in the present.

This is less complicated and more instinctive than it sounds. The flash of realisation and recognition can often come before you have even focused on the process you are going through. And the recognition itself is often enough to clear the way for the calmness, confidence or other positive resource to be reached and enjoyed.

6 ways to be more flexible

The basic idea summed up in the NLP precept 'If what you're doing isn't working, do something different' seems so obvious that you would imagine everyone would realise it and act on it all the time. Most people don't. In practice, they often take one of two other, equally unproductive courses – they redouble their efforts and do more of what's not working, or they spend time and energy defending their position, justifying their approach and trying to convince the world there was never any alternative.

What would help most in these circumstances is often a large dose of flexibility. But how do you make yourself more flexible? NLP can suggest a number of techniques that take the desire for more flexibility out of the realms of wishful thinking and into the domain of positive action. Here are six of the best:

1. Develop flexibility by learning from those who already have it.

As with most desirable qualities, one of the best ways to acquire flexibility is to emulate and learn from those who have it. You can even ask them how they do it, though you must be prepared to supplement what they tell you they do with your own observations of how they really act, as the two are not always the same. Pick your models of flexibility according to your needs, bearing in mind that being flexible encompasses a whole range of different qualities. Some people are good at crossword puzzles and have the particular kind of intellectual agility that enjoys such mental gymnastics. Others possess a specialised kind of flexibility that can, for example, show up in the way they avoid getting stuck in trench warfare situations in their personal relationships. There are many other types of flexibility that could be useful to you. Maybe they require different skills – and you need to know what they are. If you find people with the skills you need, you can observe and question them and even, perhaps, get them involved in coaching you to develop the skills they have.

2. Increase your flexibility by freeing yourself from limiting beliefs.

Whenever you say 'I ought to' do something, or use expressions like 'have to', 'can't', 'should' or 'must never', you are revealing the presence in your world of limiting beliefs. Once you start noticing them, every instance helps reveal to you what you believe is not possible, for yourself or for others. When other people use these terms, they are telling you of their beliefs about how the world is and about the ways those limiting beliefs restrict the choice of options available to them. All generalised 'rules' should be scrutinised carefully – including, of course, this one. Whenever you find yourself thinking 'I should ...', stop yourself right there. Ask yourself, 'What would happen if I didn't?' If you think it through and find that nothing much would happen, as is often the case, you will suddenly be aware of having a lot more room to manoeuvre. And if you hear someone (or yourself) saying 'I can't ...', ask yourself 'What stops me?'

3. Exercise your flexibility by putting yourself in new environments and new situations.

When the chance to do something new or go somewhere different comes up, start by assuming you'll say yes to the opportunity. Some people walk around all the time with an unconscious filter between them and the world that only lets them see the downside risks in a new situation. This isn't cool. It isn't even realistic, as the vast majority of things we worry about never happen. If you place yourself in new experiences, you stimulate yourself. Often, new ideas and new answers can then arise and you are more able to achieve an unflustered adaptability that lets you make the most of your personal and other resources.

4. Practise your flexibility by examining your routines and habits with an open mind.

Knowing what you now know about what you want from life, do your daily and weekly routines make sense? Do they help you move closer to your goals? Suppose you had a Martian pen-friend to whom you had confided all your hopes and dreams over the years. If he arrived tomorrow, knowing all your hopes and fears but nothing about the conventions of Earthling life, would he understand why you live the way you do?

5. To achieve social flexibility, be curious about other people.

If someone is aggressive or unpleasant towards you, let your curiosity focus on how it is possible for anyone to be obnoxious like this and what that behaviour can possibly be doing for that person's benefit. Ask yourself, 'How does he (or she) do that?' The more curious you are, the less reactive you will be. Reactivity is the enemy of flexibility, because it is the triggering of a highly rehearsed set of responses ('Faced with this stimulus, I always do this'). When you become curious, instead of snapping straight into your rehearsed response you are engaging with what's happening in a quite different way. And you can be curious about almost anything. In the case of offensive people, don't just get annoyed at the crass behaviour. Ask yourself questions like, 'How do they do it?', 'Do they always do it?' and 'What might happen if the response was something quite different from what they normally get?' This curious, investigative approach puts you in a different relationship to the experience. You may even want to be more curious about yourself. Ask yourself: 'How come I always seem to react like that? What would it be like if I didn't?' Whatever the circumstances, the one thing you can be sure of is that a change in your reactions will change the situation, somehow. So if everyone's stuck and going nowhere, surprise them all and surprise yourself. React differently and see what happens.

6. Be flexible by borrowing a fresh perspective.

When you are facing a problem you can't solve, try getting someone else's point of view. Try thinking like a millionaire ('How would I deal with this if money was no object?'). Try pretending you are immortal ('How would I do it if I had all the time in the world?'). Pick someone you admire (real or fictional, alive or dead, it makes no difference) and imagine what they would do. How would Stephen Hawking see the problem? Or John Lennon? Or Mother Teresa, or your business competitor, or Bill Gates, or Eleanor Roosevelt, or Sherlock Holmes ... or your mum? Just inviting your brain to look at the world from these distinctly different angles challenges it to play with the idea and process it to concoct some sort of sense. Amazingly often, something wonderful happens and your mental autopilot comes back with an offbeat suggestion that you can use. This shouldn't be surprising, as the human brain is flexibility personified, as well as being vastly more powerful than any computing device we can dream of building. It is mighty, associative and tireless, and can come up with endless ideas with effortless ease. So keep going. Don't just take on one other viewpoint and stick with that. Nothing changes the world like a change of perspective – and you can try on as many as you wish, free of charge.

When you choose, you manage

Successful people – by any measure you like – have a very strong tendency to shape their lives and manage the situations around them. Others prove that they have the potential to do this, but then go and get it all wrong. They do it in one domain, managing their business careers superbly, for example, and then losing the initiative by letting all the rest of their life fall apart. The most fulfilled people actively shape the different aspects of their lives, personal and professional, to get what they want out of their time.

'Ah,' you may say. 'That's all very well if you are rich and powerful and in a position to call the shots and tell people what to do.' But it is important to realise that this is not something that is simply the privilege of the wealthy and the leisured. A person can be extravagantly wealthy and still totally unfulfilled. The converse is also true: however little you feel you have and whatever your external circumstances, you can start managing your life now, from the inside out, as long as you have a few of the basic tools you need to help you do it.

Managing yourself, your life and other people is all about recognising that you have far more choice than you previously thought. The truth is simple: managing is about choosing.

Every time you make a choice, you have the opportunity to manage some aspect or other of the situation you are in. Take, for example, the familiar situation of driving in heavy traffic. It doesn't matter whether it's the M25 or the Los Angeles freeway or the nightly crawl along some local road. If you can choose to manage your internal state so that you are not rattled and irritated by a traffic jam you can do nothing to solve, you will have a far less fraught and frustrated journey. It may be easier said than done, but look at the way some people start to get themselves steamed up about the expectation of heavy traffic before they even know, for certain, how bad the going will be. That doesn't help at all. Simply refusing to accept this kind of anticipation – saying to yourself 'OK, it's sometimes bad, but let's see what it's like tonight', rather than fretting and fuming in advance – can be the start of a real improvement.

Sometimes the road will be a nightmare, but sometimes, too, it will be running inexplicably freely. The anticipation that things will be bad, that it will rain on the wedding day, that the fish won't bite and that you won't see eye to eye with your new boss, is not only unhelpful – it is positively harmful. It marks you out as a victim, because you will suffer stress and anxiety, even on the days when the sun keeps shining and the road is clear.

Pessimism isn't cool. It's corrosive and demoralising, and it involves you in denying the partial control that you can, very profitably, exercise over your own state and moods.

You can't mope when your pulse is racing

If, for example, you choose to do something vigorous, like running or swimming, when you are in a pessimistic mood or inclined towards anticipatory anxiety, it will have a remarkably clear-cut effect. It will alter your metabolic rate – and, with it, your state. You can't mope when your pulse is racing. You can't swim and fret at the same time. The choice you exercise in deciding to swim or run is a decision to adjust yourself towards a more resourceful state from which to handle your problems.

What appears to be a choice concerning actions is actually – and more importantly – a choice concerning your state. It works the other way round, too, because what alters your physiology always alters your state, for better or for worse. Have you noticed how unsatisfying it can sometimes be to take a day off and do nothing? It ought to be a pleasure, a delightful break from the pressures and hurly-burly of your normal schedule. Yet some days spent lazing around can leave you feeling as tired as you were before. Doing what you enjoy is invigorating and empowering. Doing nothing can sometimes do nothing for you. The secret, as always, is to manage yourself, to be aware of how to take control and then do it, so that you get what you want and need out of your time and your life.

PART II

The Life Course

Chapter 5

Beginnings

Once begun, a task is easy; half the work is done.

Horace

When did the war start?

Do you remember what you were doing the day war broke out? Which war? Well, what about the Gulf War? When the Gulf conflict suddenly flared into life in 1991, after months of posturing and brinkmanship, it seemed to amaze everyone. Its beginning was dramatic and spectacular. Yet it was a strange phenomenon: the war with a beginning and an end, but no middle. In a few days, it was all over, amid a sense of anticlimax that would have been more appropriate for a play or a film than a conflict that cost thousands of lives. But the fact that it was all beginning, an instantaneous event that started with a bang and was history within a week, made it strangely appropriate for our times.

By contrast, half a century earlier, the Second World War was the war that never seemed start. It began in September 1939, with Hitler's tanks rolling across Poland. Trenches were dug in

London's Hyde Park as Britons got out the gas masks, evacuated their children to supposedly safe parts of the country and waited for the first air raids. But not only were there no raids for several months after that, there was also virtually no sign that the war had begun. The period known as the Phoney War was not phoney for the Poles, nor for many other people across Europe. But for the British it was a strange, eerie experience that only ended with the horror of the Luftwaffe's first concerted bombing raids in early 1940. The lack of a clear beginning to the war created a sense of unreality. Though war had actually been declared on 3 September 1939, the real beginning only came when the war threatened people with immediate and deadly consequences.

It is no accident that today's war should be so much more sudden and explosive in its onset, with so much more emphasis on a sharply focused beginning. We live in an age that is very keen on abrupt beginnings and jump-cut edits, in-your-face television and insistent newness in every field.

In our parents' lifetime, the new technologies that excited people were to do with big science and big projects – things like atomic energy, space travel and Concorde, that scarcely touched the lives of ordinary people. Now we have mobile phones and faxes, computers at home and airbags in our cars, and all these new inventions are right here as part of our daily routines. We have a taste for novelty and an addiction to beginnings that is almost physical. Even those people who watch cricket aren't so keen on the slow pace of five-day Test matches any more – there's too much middle and not enough beginning and ending. As a generation, we like the sort of beginning that gets the adrenalin sluicing around the body, because of excitement, fear or first-night nerves, rather than a long, gradual build-up. But, as individuals, we still have a lot of different approaches to beginnings and it can be very useful to be aware of your own habits and prejudices, so that you can work with them – rather than against them – to manage this aspect of your life.

In this chapter, we will be drawing on the NLP techniques and insights that will help you manage the beginnings in your life. Given that everybody's life is inevitably made up of a lot of over-lapping beginnings, transitions and endings, having a range of techniques for handling and controlling them makes managing yourself and managing your life a great deal easier and more comfortable.

Absolute beginners and total non-starters

Some people are very keen on beginnings. They like to begin new projects. They like the start of a new relationship or the forma-tion of a new business. They like to start rebuilding cars, designing Web sites, writing songs, painting rooms or learning languages, whether or not all these things will ever be completed with the same joy and enthusiasm. They like the kick-off and the starting gun, the overture and the wedding bells.

Others find beginnings altogether more troubling. They linger over the planning and worry about all the little things that might go wrong. They do not relish the uncertainty that is built into every beginning. They are quite happy to let someone else take the lead and set the ball rolling, even though they may then step in to take over the management and completion of the project.

Neither of these sets of attitudes is right or wrong. But you need to know how you are with beginnings, so you can start to go for more of what works for you. After all, the art of living comfortably in the real world is largely a question of knowing enough about yourself to be able to play to your strengths and sidestep your weaknesses.

How to make beginnings easier

If you tend to get anxious about beginnings, recognising this gives you the option to manage the situation. Always going out of your way to avoid facing new situations and meeting new people can itself be extremely stressful and is obviously deeply flawed as a long-term strategy for life. But that doesn't mean there's nothing you can do about your dislike of starting things. In fact, there are several practical steps you can take to manage the situation when what seems like a daunting beginning looms in your life:

1. Make sure you are closely supported.

If your friends and loved ones can't be there for you at the time, make sure they are available before and after.

2. Ensure you are adequately prepared.

This will take your mind off your feelings in advance, help you feel that you deserve a successful outcome and equip you to make that outcome more likely.

3. Use the three-step technique to take control of your state by re-living past success.

Now is the time to put into practice the simple three-step technique for making yourself positive and resourceful that you learned earlier (see Chapter 4). Just identify the ideal state for dealing with this situation, recall a past occasion when you have been in precisely that state and re-live it as vividly as you can, activating all the specific sights, sounds, feelings and smells associated in your memory with your past triumph.

4. Move the goalposts, so that what's troubling you is no longer seen as a beginning.

To see how this works, take the example of writer's block. Writer's block is seldom a block to writing absolutely anything at all. It is frequently more a problem over getting started. So forget the beginning. Start writing – or tidying up or doing your accounts or whatever else you have to do – at some arbitrary middling point and do what supposedly has to come first later on.

5. Stand everything on its head and see the novelty of the situation as a bonus for you.

If you are going to spot a new business idea, meet a new friend or learn something you didn't know before, it won't usually happen within your usual round of routine tasks and everyday people. Instead of feeling that the new is happening to you, shift the locus of control back inside you by asking yourself questions that mean you engage with what's happening on your terms. So instead of walking into a party or a conference and thinking 'Oh no, I don't know anyone here,' think, 'There's going to be someone I can gain by knowing in any group of people – how am I going to find that person here?'

Not everyone finds beginnings difficult to manage. At the other extreme, there are many people who use beginnings and exploit them, more or less consciously, as tools in their lives and careers.

Some use small beginnings to energise themselves; if they're down in the dumps, they'll deliberately launch a new project to kickstart their zest for life. For those people, even opening a new packet of biscuits or breaking the seal of a fresh jar of instant coffee can bring a momentary boost to a dull day. You have probably witnessed, too, the way some people take the opportunity of a new beginning to reinvent themselves, with a new persona and perhaps even a radically rewritten life history for the benefit of a new job or a fresh circle of acquaintances.

Even if the story of your life is not rewritten for a new audience, the fact that you are relating it to the interests of a new group of people provides ample opportunity to choose what spin you put on the tale – what you put in, what you leave out and what you exaggerate for comic or tragic effect. No one knows the whole truth about anyone, anyway. A new beginning gives you the chance to reposition the product – you – just a little closer to the person you would like to be.

The weekend starts here

In the 1960s, in the heady days of 'Swinging London', the top UK pop programme on television used to be *Ready, Steady, Go*. Every Friday evening, the presenter, Cathy MacGowan, would peer out from beneath her fringe and trill 'The weekend starts here', as if officially consecrating the next fifty-three hours to the pursuit of music, parties and pleasure. The funny thing was that, for a whole generation of teenagers, it really worked. Once those four magic words had been spoken, it did seem as if the watershed between school or work and what really mattered had been crossed. A beginning had been marked and celebrated, and reality would be put on hold until Monday morning broke the spell.

The trick that *Ready, Steady, Go* managed to pull off was to make a particular time early on Friday evenings seem like a real beginning, when it was really just the slot the planners had chosen for the screening of the show. There was no reason at all why the line should have been drawn at 6.30 or 7 or 8 o'clock, other than the schedulers' decision. Yet the difference between drifting into the weekend and having it formally announced was highly significant. It introduced a sense of ceremony, as much a ritual, in its own way, as the old tradition of firing off the noonday gun in colonial Hong Kong once was.

Ceremonies and rituals have always been used to emphasise the grandeur of beginnings, when there is a monarch to be crowned, a ship to be launched, a New Year to be rung in or a wedding to be celebrated. But as life, generally, has become less formal, the scale of the rituals has changed. They are smaller and less expansive, and people are less clear about the etiquette involved. But there are just as many rituals now as there ever have been. The ritual beginning when you meet someone may have changed from 'How do you do?' to 'Hi' or 'Hello', but it hasn't disappeared. In some countries fewer people now exchange formal handshakes, but if you watch closely you'll observe that many still like to make some fleeting physical contact, perhaps touching the other person's arm as they speak, as if wanting to register that a real 'live' meeting has occurred and some sort of new relationship has been started.

In the past, the framework imposed by a more formal code of manners and behaviour went some way towards masking the individual's reaction to many situations involving beginnings. Today that cover is largely gone. A more spontaneous, improvising culture is bound to mean that people have to work out their own ways of handling work and social beginnings. Where etiquette no longer provides stock answers, you'll find NLP really useful in helping you handle things flexibly and successfully.

How to get off to a good start with anyone

Sometimes you are introduced to someone you just have to get on with. This is a kind of beginning many people dread. The new boss, the new sister-in-law or the new neighbour may not be someone you like the look of, yet you just can't afford to let the relationship get off to a bad start. But is there anything you can do? Well, yes, there is. Follow this technique for getting off to a good start with someone new:

1. Be clear about the outcome you want.

If you know why meeting this person, or getting on with them, matters to you, you'll be far more likely to establish a good rapport with them. People who work this way also tend to be much more flexible and resilient – key attributes for building successful social and professional relationships. They know where they are going and simply adjust their behaviour to get there, without being blown off course by any chance upset or slight. They are also much less likely to be thrown by the unexpected, because their goals remain constant.

2. Recognise the new person's talents or expertise.

You don't have to like, or trust, the whole person to recognise that someone may have real and valuable skills or knowledge. Why bother? Because we often generalise from our first impression to the whole person and this can stop us recognising other dimensions of their character and abilities that would be perfectly OK in our eyes.

3. Ensure the other person benefits from meeting you.

You can get off to a much better start with people if you are clear at the outset about what needs to have happened by the end of the meeting to make it worth while for them. Get curious.

Whether it's a personal or a professional meeting, ask yourself 'What will make the new person feel good about having met me?' If you can't think of anything, you may need more information about what's important to this person. You may need to ask yourself whether now is really the right time to meet up. And you may need to spend more time thinking about what contribution you can bring to this, or any other, party.

4. Find something to like about the new person.

Find *something* – anything at all – to like about the person. It doesn't have to be anything major or deeply significant. It doesn't have to mean anything. It could be the person's jacket or haircut or briefcase.

You may be wincing at the newcomer's abrasive manner, but if you can focus on one positive feature, it will save you from the fundamental mistake of seeing the new person as a caricature, wholly unpleasant or 100 per cent negative.

How do you keep the spark alive?

If some people find every beginning potentially threatening, there are others for whom beginnings become a habitual response to adversity. 'When I get bogged down, I know I sometimes like to make a break and award myself a new beginning' one entrepreneur told us. He had a good excuse for this, because he had tried to build up companies in several different industry sectors and been thwarted, each time, by elements that could justifiably be seen to be outside his control.

But the tendency to want to make a break and start all over again can be addictive. It can be a neat strategy to extricate yourself from failure and give yourself the impetus of a new start. It can also be much more negative – more a question of always jumping ship and never having the bottle to see things through to completion.

For the great majority of people whose liking for beginnings stops far short of addiction, there are ways of keeping the spark alive. The trick with relationships, for example, is to keep that keen, edgy sense of newness and unpredictability going over a long period.

When an intimate relationship begins, it is naturally new, fresh and highly charged – exciting or scary or possibly both. Whatever happens next, over the following weeks, months or years, love and attraction may remain strong but the original newness, the sense of being right at the very beginning of something unique and unknown, is slowly diluted. Part of the secret of keeping the relationship young is to make it continue to feel new by introducing new beginnings.

People understand this instinctively when they plan their holidays so that they can go to new places together or try activities they have never experienced before. But holidays are among the big set-pieces in people's lives, taking up relatively few days each year and often loading the participants with a great deal of organisational stress. Introducing a culture of new beginnings into the day-to-day texture of your life, with little adventures, minor surprises and unexpected deviations from the usual routes and routines, is a more practical approach to sustainable newness.

Don't wait for the alarm call

For those who manage this aspect of their lives cleverly – and those with a natural gift of enthusiasm and optimism – every day is a new beginning. But another group of people who tend to feel the truth of this are those who arc conscious of living on borrowed time. It is all too often the first heart attack or some other equally brutal wake-up call that makes people refocus their priorities and reshape their thinking to begin living for the day. But why wait for the bad news? If your behaviour would be very different if you had only six months to live, isn't it worth investigating what you could do to get more of that vivid urgency and vitality into the life you're leading now?

Most of us live lives that are less than ideal, by our own, highly personalised standards. Perhaps, though, we're too undemanding for our own good. Why not begin, now, to do a great deal more of what you enjoy most?

However many retirement parties you go to, you don't meet many sixty-five-year-olds who say, 'You know, I wish I'd spent more of my life at the office.' At the same time, we do meet a surprising number of young people in their teens and early twenties who don't seem to be getting as much out of their youth and freedom as they feel they should. Young and old, there are certainly too many people around who are very far from seeing each new day as a beginning that can give them new pleasures, new experiences and new opportunities to enjoy themselves.

No limits – what do you really like doing?

One way of getting to grips with how you might begin to get more out of your life is to focus on what gives you pleasure, excitement and satisfaction. There may be some new beginnings that are needed here. Take a few minutes now and write yourself a wildly uninhibited, impractical, unconstrained list of five wishes. What five things would you do if there were no limits, no rules and you knew you couldn't fail?

Don't think twice. Just do it. Even if you have chosen to put off trying some of the other exercises in the book until later, this one is so important that you should not wait. But you must stick strictly to the terms of the question. No limits and no risk of failure, for example, means that you are not allowed to leave things off your list because of all the usual mundane practical reasons like 'It's impossible', 'It would cost a fortune', 'I wouldn't be good enough' or 'I'd need the co-operation of too many other people'. Forget all those constraints and explore the outer limits of your wishes and desires. No rules, too, means no consequences, no punishments – not even any reproaches. In a world without laws of humanity or nature, what would you do? If the world and everyone in it were entirely dedicated to your pleasure, excitement and satisfaction, what would you want? It's a strange and powerful mental experiment, to glimpse your universe in such stark, raw colours, but it can tell you things about yourself that are normally kept well hidden. Don't hesitate. Do it now.

Five things I would do if there were no limits, no rules and I couldn't fail:

1. ....

2. ....

3. ....

4. ....

5. ....

It is important to understand that you are under no compulsion to act on any or all of the insights you gain from doing this. The exercise may have uncovered unexpected aspects of your wants and your frustrations, but there is no need to be unnerved by them. It is up to you what use you make of the information. But it can, if the circumstances demand it, help you change your life.

We know one young manager for whom doing this exercise, more than ten years ago, was quite literally a turning point. He had respectability, a good job and an enviable income, an impressive car, home, marriage and a future. What he discovered he wanted, from this and related exercises, was quite different. He wanted independence, in a big way, but he had been suppressing this because of all the commitments he had already made. His suppressed wishes included wanting to work for himself, to become a musician, to travel the world, to pursue his fantasies of a life of sex and drugs and rock 'n' roll and to live in the sun, far from the grey skies of the northern European winter. Bit by bit, in close collaboration with his wife, who had seen how frustrated he was becoming in his old life, he began to make plans and make changes. They agreed that their relationship was of paramount importance and that fidelity was not negotiable. Beyond that, however, he was amazed to find that his wife was happy to go along with a complete change of lifestyle. They are now in Australia and still together. He runs a yacht chandlery in a harbour opposite the Great Barrier Reef and plays in an Irish folk group and both he and his wife are delighted with the new life they have made for themselves.

For this couple, the 'No Limits' process was a catalyst, helping to bring to the surface desires and dreams that would have demanded attention anyway, at some point. It ensured that the need for a rethink was brought into focus early enough for both partners to develop a plan together. All too often, it is not like that – one partner has wishes and frustrations that remain secret and suppressed until the pressure builds up and there is an explosion that can just blow things apart. Your 'No Limits' list is a valuable part of the toolkit for managing your life.

Now write yourself a second list. What have you been missing out on? Again, the emphasis is on actions – doing things, rather than possessing objects – because what people like to do with their time and their energy is usually far more revealing than what they would like to own. So, now, what five things do you regret not having done – or done enough of – in your life?

Five things I haven't done enough of in my life (so far):

1. ....

2. ....

3. ....

4. ....

5. ....

Both these lists may be revealing in themselves. But what will probably be most revealing of all is the way they highlight different aspects of your wants and desires. We have yet to run this exercise with anyone whose two lists covered exactly the same ground, though they might seem, at first glance, to be responding to almost the same questions. In the nooks and crannies between these two lists, you can often find real clues to your own motivation and frustrations – and strong hints as to how you can make a start on getting more of what you really want.

If you are not already actively seeking the opportunity to do the things you want to do, what's stopping you? Just going through these exercises could be one of the most constructive things you've ever done. It can be disconcerting – especially if you have managed to be unflinchingly honest about what's lacking in your present experience of life – but it's still guaranteed to be a lot less threatening than going through the cautionary experience of a heart attack. You don't need to wait for the alarm call. You can begin living more fully now.

Chapter 6

Transitions

A permanent state of transition is Man's most noble condition.

Juan Ramón Jímenez

Making the necessary changes

Imagine what your life would be like if it turned out to be the same throughout, consistent from beginning to end.

People are funny about change. Many fear it. Yet the most profound changes of all are the transitions that are part of everyone's life. One way to understand your life better is to develop an understanding of the key phases you go through and the way they affect you. Something like adolescence is an obvious stage of transition, as you move from dependent child to independent adult. But you've known other, equally significant, changes. What about the shock to the system when you first entered the adult world of work?

The key transitions invariably require a period of adjustment afterwards – and may need advance preparation, too, either conscious or unconscious – however quickly they seem to happen. Without these transitions, your life would be static, boring and staid and you would inevitably remain undeveloped as a person. Every transition brings change, sometimes feared, sometimes longed for. But even the ardently desired changes – leaving school, marriage, promotion and so on – still present challenges. Even the giant steps forward can have a downside or force you to make compromises. The process of adjusting to the new is part of what makes a life transition.

Whose marriage are you in?

Take getting married. Almost everyone embarks on marriage in a spirit of optimism, even if it is not for the first time. But marriage is not just something that happens at a certain time and place on a certain day. It is a process, as well as an event. And it absolutely demands that you should make creative adjustments, if you are really going to engage in the experience of being married to someone and make that experience your own.

To talk about people failing to make the experience of marriage their own may sound strange. But you have probably come across people who have got married and merely aped their parents' styles of living. In a changing world, both generations and individuals have to remake the idea of marriage for their own times and personalities. If you live in a borrowed idea of marriage, rather than renewing and reinventing it for yourself, it should be no surprise if you find that you are less than content with the results.

In the corporate arena, the nearest equivalent to a marriage is a merger. Sometimes there is a meeting of minds, sometimes a shotgun in the background. But the biggest challenge for management, throughout the transitional period, is usually the coming together of alien cultures. WH Smith buys a trendy

Internet bookseller. Smart-suited IBM merges with chinos-clad Lotus. Commercial Union ties the knot with General Accident. In each case, whether the business marriage is seen as a merger or a simple takeover of one company by another, those who are charged with running the enlarged business cannot afford to let hostility, resentment and 'them and us' attitudes put the brakes on future performance.

Somehow, ways have to be found to make the experience of the new company belong to all those working in it, whichever side of the family they originally came from. When it comes to merging cultures, managing transition is something that feeds straight through into company performance.

Be it two people or two companies coming together, the first rule is not to let one partner's culture or lifestyle swamp the other partner's contribution. The key to making this work is to pick out and emphasise some of the history, habits and strands of tradition that each side brings to the relationship and utilise them as elements in the creation of something new and different.

When Jeremy and Liz decided they wanted to be together more they chose to live together. It seemed pretty straightforward. They were both sensible people and so looked at who had the more living space. Liz's apartment was bigger and more central, so Jeremy moved in and that became their new home. But it never really worked. In Jeremy's words, 'Although Liz tried to make space for my things I still felt it was her place. At best I was a guest. Sometimes I felt more like a lodger.' Liz was hurt by this and didn't feel Jeremy was really committed to being in a full-time relationship. After a year they split up.

When Judy and Phil decided to live together, they realised Judy's flat wasn't big enough and Phil's was in a part of town where Judy wouldn't feel comfortable. The solution was for both of them to move into a new place together. 'It was the best thing we could have done' Judy says. Phil agrees: 'It meant we started afresh. It was our place, not hers or mine.'

Taking the initiative

In career terms, too, knowing what you want and making sure you are driving your own career, rather than just following in other people's footsteps, will always be vital factors if you want to manage your life effectively. The course of your working life will be determined by a number of key moments when you have the power to shape your own destiny.

In 1978, Ian McDermott was wanting to become self-employed and set up his own business. Recognising that this was likely to be a significant transition, needing preparation, action and a period of adjustment afterwards, he invented a half-way house for himself by taking on a short-term, one-year contract. This decision gave him a temporary source of income and a new working environment in which to develop his career strategy. At the same time, the short contract ruled out getting too comfortable in the new lifestyle and set a deadline for further decisive action. For a full twelve months, while he went about his daily business, Ian's mind was doing a mass of conscious and unconscious processing, mulling over thoughts and ideas about how he should act once the contract ended and he was out on his own, with no safety net.

The careful pacing of this transition paid real dividends. Changing jobs is often quite unnerving in itself. Switching from the predictability of a full-time job to the uncertainties of self-employment can be very demanding, not least because it requires adjustments to one's self-image and, ideally, the development of an unsinkable belief in oneself.

By deliberately making time for both the conscious and the unconscious to get to grips with the desired change, Ian utilised the full range of his mental resources to prepare for it. Long before his personal D-day arrived, he was full of ideas and energy and itching to put his plans into action. What could have been a disconcerting change of circumstances became part of a wider drive towards a set of compelling and clearly visualised goals. By managing the nature of the transition process and controlling its pace, it was possible to stack the odds in favour of its successful completion.

Transitions are where you shape your life

This business of remaking common or universal experiences so that they fit in with your personality, goals and beliefs does not only apply to marriage and career shifts. It tends to come to the fore with all the significant transitions in people's lives. For example, emotionally and biologically (not to mention economically), there is nothing in life to compare with the transition from being childless to having children. As soon as you have your first child, you are faced with the question, 'What kind of a family are you going to create?' On the face of it, the transition is instantaneous. The person who says, even one day beforehand, 'I am about to become a parent' is a different person from the one who sits there twenty-four hours later thinking, 'This is my baby.' The change is complete and irreversible. But the period of adjustment may take years.

Transitions give people their chances to tailor-make their own lives. Faced with the option of settling for an off-the-peg life that fits where it touches or setting your sights on the Savile Row version, it is sometimes easy to convince yourself that you can't – or don't deserve to – have the life you want. You can, though. And what's more, you *do* deserve it. Once you know what you want and are prepared to recognise how much you are responsible for what you get, you can use the opportunities offered by change and transition to steer yourself towards your goals.

How to spot a real transition

In order to get to grips with the nature of transitions, try this exercise. It will help you chart, in a way you may not have done before, the way the sequence of events in your life has helped to shape the person you have become.

The Transition Tracker

1. *Take a piece of paper and write down a list of ten of the most important turning points in your life.*

2. *When you have noted down ten specific experiences, ask yourself these questions about each of the turning points you have listed.*
   (a) Were you thinking about the experience ahead of time?
   (b) Did it seem momentous when it was actually happening?
   (c) Did it take some getting used to, after the event?
   (d) How long did the period of adjustment last?

As you look over your answers, consider how these experiences have helped to shape your life and make you the person you are today. Do you notice any patterns emerging? For example, you may recognise that these transitions always seem to happen to you, rather than being initiated by your own actions and decisions. Or you may notice that they all seemed oddly anticlimactic at the time and only seemed to take on their true significance afterwards. If there are recognisable patterns, being aware of them will give you important clues about what to watch out for and when to intervene to manage future transitions more successfully.

To manage your life, manage your transitions

It is important to recognise that we are all different. For each of us, particular things that are happening will carry unique and personal significance. There are people for whom a fortieth birthday feels like one of life's great watersheds. There are others – perhaps friends and colleagues – for whom nothing could be less significant than the numbers on the calendar or the birthday cards.

One person's turning points may be just everyday occurrences to someone else. Yet there are some events that we can all recognise as the big ones. And part of what gives them this universal importance is the sort of transition they signify. Learning to drive, passing your test and getting your first driving licence, for example, is as much a rite of passage for modern, urban youth as any tribal coming-of-age ritual.

As the non-driving, dependent child turns into the licensed, independent adult, a moment is passed which exactly meets all the criteria for a true transition, from the long and conscious period of preparation, to the even longer, and largely subconscious, period of adjustment and consolidation after the formal turning point. But it is not only the young driver who is likely to be going through a major transition. Mobility is bestowed on the youngster, along with a new freedom to pay for the petrol it demands. Freedom is bestowed on the parents, along with a new obligation to worry and fret each evening until their ex-child is safely home. If you care enough, other people's transitions can be just as demanding for you.

It is obvious that some of these life transitions can be planned in, slotting into fixed dates in the diary of your life. Others come at you out of the blue, unpredictably and without giving you the opportunity to gear up for them. Strangely enough, though, whether they are expected or not often makes little difference to the impact they have on your life. *It is how you react to them that tends to matter most.*

By the time you have finished this chapter, you will have several new NLP techniques at your disposal to put you more firmly in the driving seat. And when you know how to manage these events in ways that work for you, you will feel more at ease with yourself and more at ease in the world. You will certainly be more in charge of your destiny than most people – and better able to be yourself and trust in your own responses.

Plan to make change happen on your terms

The main reason for looking at how you are with transitions is so that you understand the territory you inhabit and stand a better chance of being able to manage what's going on. Many people are all too used to the feeling of being on the receiving end of change – and they just don't feel good about it. What is needed is a set of practical ways to adjust the structure of your life, so that you can incorporate change and transition and make them work for you, on your behalf.

You can begin to do it, in relation to events and transitions that lie ahead, by planning how you will handle them. If you look at the major transitions that most of us are likely to go through

– experiences of birth, death and marriage, for example, affecting ourselves or those immediately around us – you can see many of these coming, some time in advance. If you identify these future transitions now, you can start deciding how you intend to engage with them when they arrive.

You can't control your world. But you can decide what kind of twenty-first, fortieth or sixtieth birthday you want and what you will choose to let it mean to you.

You may not be able to guarantee keeping your present job, but you can start figuring out, now, how you'd handle things if you needed to find another job – and what, specifically, you would be looking for.

Is a new baby going to be seen as an awesome responsibility or a chance to do all sorts of young and silly things, with the child as an alibi – or both? Is your retirement from work going to be an end or a beginning? Is your fiftieth birthday going to be a wake or a riot?

On the whole, life is not black and white. Most changes are double-edged. There are new opportunities and maybe the loss of the old familiar ways. But to a much larger extent than people tend to think, you can choose how to handle the transition.

Be clear what you want to happen

If you have already decided how you'd like things to be in times of transition and what you want particular changes to mean to you, you start off with a huge advantage. If you haven't, the first thing to do is to sort out what you would like to happen when things start to change.

Ask yourself three questions to help pull your planning into sharp focus, starting with the inevitable touchstone question that lies at the heart of so many of NLP's insights about life management:

1. 'What do you want?'
2. 'What would you enjoy?'
3. 'What would give this particular transition meaning and value for you?'

Many people never get round to thinking about what they want from life as a whole or even from little bits of it. Others have a fear of seeming selfish that lays down a barrier of taboos between them and what they truly desire or enjoy. But getting what you want really does start with knowing what that might be.

If you can be clear about what a good result for you would be, you begin to stand a chance of getting it. Transitions are necessarily times of change – and where there's change, there are opportunities for things to go well or badly and for you to influence them in one direction or the other. What is going to help you make the most of these opportunities? Or perhaps, if the transition you are going through is unwelcome, it may be more helpful to see the question in rather different terms.

Unwelcome transitions

For people who are adopting the crash position and bracing themselves for the onset of unwelcome transitions, the key questions becomes: 'What can you do to make yourself more resourceful in these new circumstances?' The answers come in many forms.

1. Make time for you.

Give yourself a time and place to step back to prepare. The key word here is *prepare*. It's no good giving yourself time if you use it to stare at the television. You may just be avoiding thinking about what is to come. If there's no time to draw breath and you're racing headlong towards change, it's very easy to feel out of control and at the mercy of external forces. If you're going to be in the driving seat, you have to give yourself time.

You may choose to do this on your own or with help from someone else. Much of the most useful work in executive coaching involves enabling people to find the resources they need within themselves to handle the transitions they are facing. Very often people need to step out of the hurly-burly to do this – which is why Ian McDermott always sees clients for executive coaching away from their office.

Often they find that the crucial piece is not out there in the external world at all, but on the inside. As one finance director put it: 'I needed to change the limiting beliefs I had about myself before I could really step into my new post. Until then, I didn't feel I was up to the challenge.'

2. Talk to someone who has been through it before.

The very fact that other people have been there too can make their advice, or even just their concern, of special value. There are times when you need to talk things over, not with an expert or a professional but with an ordinary person whose only qualification is a shared experience.

But there is also another, physiological dimension that is equally important.

3. Give yourself some hibernation time.

Award yourself as much sleep as you can fit in and feel comfortable with. Big changes make big demands on the psyche. They can destabilise your natural mode of functioning and make you vulnerable to infection and illness. A lot of mental processing goes on while you are asleep and it is also the time when your body revives and fortifies itself. Rediscovering the healing power of sleep is something every person and every generation seems to have to do all over again, but all the ideas about it that Shakespeare put into Macbeth's mouth 400 years ago are still true – 'sore labour's bath, balm of hurt minds . . . chief nourisher in life's feast'. Recent research has been very clear about the important role sleep plays in strengthening and recharging the immune system. Combined with its importance as a time for offline processing of thoughts and ideas, this all points to the unique restorative value of sleep and dreaming.

4. Pay attention to diet, exercise and physical well-being.

Diet
When you are anxious or troubled, your appetite can go a bit haywire. For some people, the stop signals from body to brain that tell you when you've had enough become muted, confused or very slow. If this happens, the secret is to eat slowly to allow time for the message to percolate up. Delay the repeated impulse to take another bite or two. For other people, the opposite problem occurs and all appetite for food vanishes. The trick here is to decide on something you can get on and do in relation to the change that is affecting you and then eat little and often, so that you have the fuel you need to go forward.

Exercise

Get active and you'll change your brain chemistry and the way you feel, both physically and emotionally. This can help you manage your inner state even as you build your physical resilience. You'll feel that you have more stamina – and it won't just be physical.

Physical well-being

Make sure you get whatever gives you a sense of physical well-being. Don't dismiss little things. They often provide the greatest comfort. Take feet for instance. One woman said that having a regular pedicure got her through her divorce because she felt cared for at the time and good about herself afterwards!

5. Create a comforting project.

For many people there is great comfort to be found in activity. So another way of resourcing yourself is to *do* something. This something will have more structure and be more sustainable if you actually make it a project.

It may be something you've wanted to do for ages or be quite different from anything you've ever done before. It's up to you. When her youngest child finally flew the nest Jan became very low. Her solace was to do something for herself – for the next year she threw herself into learning Italian. She still missed her children, but in her words, 'I was starting to make a new life by finding a new love, and my enthusiasm helped me through.'

6. Pick a perspective that will work for you.

It is important not to make things unnecessarily difficult by being hard on yourself when big and disruptive changes are taking place in your life. Major transitions can sap your energy and confidence in all sorts of ways. It is not realistic to assume that you should be able to glide effortlessly through them. But recognise also that a very high proportion of the shocking, unforeseen, out-of-the-blue events that force changes upon us are neither life-threatening nor necessarily as drastic as they seem at first.

Deciding to take control of the perspective in which you view change is an important part of life management. Make a deliberate, conscious attempt to be clear about how this particular transition, welcome or unwelcome, can fit into your life, so that eventually you and your life may be the better for it. Just making the effort to do this – to make sense of things and find the pattern that links them together – is genuinely empowering and liberating.

Early in her career Ian McDermott's wife, Paulette, had a very unwelcome change thrust upon her. She was a young school social worker in a department of thirty in Connecticut. These are the people who go into the schools and make sure children are getting what they need in their lives outside school, so that they can progress well in the classroom. She and her colleagues were supervised by five senior social workers.

To reduce costs the Regional School Board simply abolished the post of school social worker. So a whole department just disappeared and thirty people were made redundant.

For Paulette and her colleagues this was a huge shock. Initially it was frightening – the question of money being the prime concern. But then she started thinking. She'd been hoping to go to graduate school and had planned to do this part-time in years to come. Maybe she could do it full time now! It was certainly the best time to do it, as there weren't any children yet. And the severance pay meant she'd have some of the funds she'd need. She talked it over with her first husband. He knew what it was like to be made redundant. They decided he'd be making enough to support them.

But that wasn't all. The group of social workers decided – as a group – that they weren't just going to fall apart. So they agreed to do something together. Each put a little of their severance pay into a common fund – and then they hired a tennis pro!

They'd agreed that something which was fun and physical would make a big difference to how they felt. Every week they'd meet and have lessons, talk about their feelings and how they felt betrayed, but at the same time they'd do something physical and have a good time.

For Paulette, this redundancy changed the course of her life. Her response to it was to enter graduate school full-time and so make her future happen sooner. She also got much better at playing tennis!

Expand the reach of your comfort zone

It is a characteristic of transitions – the ones that really matter, anyway – that they tend to take you beyond the limits of your established comfort zone. In work and life, that can be a virtue in itself – to become more flexible and find that you can handle a greater variety of inputs than you thought. Or in its most extreme form, as Nietzsche said: 'What does not kill me makes me strong'.

Being pushed far beyond our limits can be painful, but a more modest stretch almost always has a positive side to it. One of the worst aspects of being taken out of your comfort zone is the tendency to panic or become defensive when you aren't sure of your ground. But that impulse is often nothing more than a habit, perhaps left over from childhood, when everything outside our home and family circle seemed disproportionately big and threatening.

As adults, we know perfectly well that we can usually manage OK in a strange town or an unfamiliar situation. So when a particular event moves you out of the zone and into the unknown, the knee-jerk reaction that says you should dig your heels in and resist is not doing you any favours.

The key to managing this sort of situation is not to cling to what's familiar but to work at expanding your comfort zone and increasing its effective radius. NLP can help you expand the boundaries of your comfort zone if you follow these tips:

Tip 1. Aim to be resourceful, not just comfortable.

Don't think of your comfort zone as an area where everything is perfect and physically comfortable all the time. If that was it, it would sometimes be a very small area indeed. A more helpful way of looking at it is to think of it as the zone within which you feel you can, generally speaking, handle whatever crops up. You won't always know what is going to happen next, but in this area you feel competent and resourceful enough to deal with most things that occur. And it's the resourcefulness, the 'I can handle it' feeling, that makes you feel comfortable.

So consider what helps you to be resourceful. Do certain activities strengthen you and give you confidence? Who are the people who can support you? Where, geographically, are you at your most resourceful? Can you spend some time there? What information do you need to either quell your fears or promote a sense of well-being?

Tip 2. Be clear about the skills you bring to this transition.

In a new role, there may well be aspects of the situation that make you feel uncomfortable, whether you're a first-time mother suddenly responsible for a newborn infant or a manager with a whole new department to run. New responsibilities and different tasks to handle can sometimes make you wonder if you have got yourself into a situation where you are going to spend most of your time outside your comfort zone.

In truth, though, you almost certainly bring some skills to the situation, and it's useful – not least for your morale – to know what these are. They are your base camp.

Tip 3. Let the familiar provide some respite.

Often it is also possible for you to find a place of safety, sometimes physical but more often emotional, that you can retreat to temporarily when the transition into the new role seems too abrupt or too demanding. If you are in danger of feeling overwhelmed and under-resourced, step back into this area and spend some time doing what brings comfort and what you know you are good at.

Tip 4. Create milestones and let each be a reward.

If you try and do it all straight away you risk being overwhelmed. Instead, manage the transition by graduating the change. Decide exactly what would make you comfortable and at home in your new role. The same sort of techniques can be used in many areas of your life, but we'll take the example of the transition into a new role at work. Suppose you have just been awarded some new managerial position. Ask yourself, 'What would it take to make me believe I really have made this transition?'

In this case that might mean: 'What would it take to make me believe I really am the manager whose title now appears against my name?' It is generally recognised that a person may need time to grow into a new job. But you can certainly accelerate that process by considering how this will happen. Ask the right questions and you will automatically lead yourself towards useful answers. Ask:

'How am I going to grow into this?'

'What steps and milestones will lead me through the transitional process?'

'Why will they be significant to me?'

If you can identify a set of appropriate milestones and attach suitable timescales to them, you can begin to manage yourself through this period of transition.

Sometimes the milestones may be pretty rough and ready. To take an extreme example, just surviving in the job for a few days or weeks may be a target in itself. Ian Shircore left university keen to be a journalist and totally unprepared for the realities of the reporter's life, even on a suburban local paper. Shocked by the lack of time available for thought or checking and horrified at being sent out to question accident victims and bereaved relatives, he was on the brink of leaving after two weeks – even though this was what he had always thought he wanted as a career.

The key to coming to terms with the job was to pace the transition carefully.

Reasoning that his holiday entitlement was four weeks and that he would have only too much time to relax if he lost the job, he booked holiday time on a two weeks on, one week off basis, to carry him through the first three months. It left him no holiday entitlement at all for the next nine months, but it did get him over the hump and started in the job. It gave him the chance to build contacts, to find a way of doing the job that he felt comfortable with, to prove there were some things he could do well and to establish himself as part of the team. Instead of losing his opportunity, Ian was able to find his bearings. He stayed at the paper for four years and still carries an NUJ card today. Pacing himself from milestone to milestone and holiday to holiday had paid off.

How to design your milestones

Generally speaking, you should aim to find or create more meaningful milestones than this. After all, simply surviving is very much a minimum standard.

If a new job requires you to develop new skills and techniques or learn your way around new equipment or processes, these can form the basis of significant milestones that will have a clearly defined factual content and may also carry personal significance for you.

Learning a new skill is always good for your confidence. By definition, it adds a little more territory to your comfort zone and gives you another resource to draw on. So your milestones will be particularly useful to you if you can shape them in a form that defines a capability, a timescale and an internal or personal reward.

What you are looking for is a milestone format that will serve your purposes. But the chances are that your milestones will also measure the sort of progress that will go down well with your employer. A formula defining your progress in terms of achievement, plus time, plus satisfaction for you, is the most powerful and motivating of all. We recommend using the form:

'By X date, I want to be able to do Y, because that will make me feel Z.'

This is an ideal format for a milestone to pace yourself through the transitional period in a new job, or in any of life's more demanding transitions.

Paulette McDermott is American and now lives in the UK. Moving continents definitely counts as a transition. These are some of the things she did to manage it.

To be resourceful she needed to prepare and orientate herself, so before she made the move she came to the UK quite a few times, just to get a feel for the country and to see what it was like. It gave her a strong sense of what kind of place she was coming to and this made a big difference. She and Ian also agreed that there would be an initial three-week period when they would be together all day, every day, after the move.

She was clear about the skills she would be bringing to this major change. From past experience she knew she was a flexible kind of person and that she could handle different ways of doing things. As a therapist, she also knew her professional skills were eminently portable and could be as easily applied in the UK as the US. But she also knew she'd need to acquire other skills such as map-reading, because the layout of roads is so different in each country.

Even though she was prepared, it was a huge change for Paulette and letting the familiar provide some respite was essential. Reconnecting to the US was one vital element: going back periodically and phoning friends and relatives as often as before was part of this. Another useful link was finding an organisation locally called the American Women of Surrey. A quite important form of the familiar, though, was creating a new home that had its own familiar aspects and objects from before. This involved a move out of London to a part of Surrey where she felt comfortable because it was much more like the New England she had left behind.

Creating the milestones was extremely important. Passing her UK driving test and achieving 'resident alien' status after the obligatory number of years were obvious and official ones. But equally important was buying the new home – new to both Ian and Paulette and their children – together and moving out of

London. Creating new traditions has also created new milestones. Every wedding anniversary is a time to go away together to somewhere new for both partners.

She was clear that by the end of the first year she wanted to know people locally, find her way around, have a private practice, be settled in the new home and enjoy sufficient time as a couple because this would make her feel it had been worth all the upheaval inside and out, and the future would follow.

That was quite a few years ago now and she's still here!

Chapter 7

Endings

Every exit is an entry somewhere else.

Tom Stoppard

Let it be

Some people just hate endings. They are troubled by goodbyes and they don't even like finishing a project they've put a lot into. But endings, like beginnings, are essential for life. If there weren't any endings, life would get extremely clogged up.

In *Gulliver's Travels* Jonathan Swift came up with the gruesome idea of the Struldbrugs, a race of people endowed with a ghastly immortality. Because they don't die, the Struldbrugs just live on, toothless, hairless, joyless, witless, for hundreds of years. They are the living dead. Swift makes it clear that these immortals are the most miserable of all races, simply because their lives don't have an ending.

The point is that endings – and even deaths – are necessary for life, for regeneration and renewal. Ripeness is all, as King Lear says. And ripeness is all about lives, relationships and many other things ending in an appropriate fashion at an appropriate time. As we shall see, a good ending is often something you can work to create and derive pride and even pleasure from. This chapter will show you how using an NLP perspective can help you create the endings you need, tie up loose ends and let go of those things from your past that you will not be needing in your future.

Good endings don't just happen

Think of a situation where you would like to move on or would like things to change. The context could be to do with work and public issues or it could be concerned with your most private and intimate relationships. But if a real need to change is there, there will always be a need for some kind of ending. To make change happen, you and others will have to let go of old ways or the old situation, as well as putting in place the new. The old will often need to be ended and closed off first, to give a new idea or system the chance to flourish. Just rushing from the old to the new always carries the risk of jumping straight from the frying pan into the fire, as anyone who has ever started a new relationship while on the rebound will testify. So part of the art of beginning afresh is finishing what you've begun and bringing what needs to be finished to a fitting conclusion. In order to get it right, you will want to ask yourself four questions in relation to your particular situation.

How to go for a good ending:

Ask yourself –

1. *'What kind of ending would make this a good ending?'*
2. *'What needs to occur so that this good ending can happen?'*

3. '*What would this look like, sound like and feel like, for me and for others?*'
4. '*What could I do to make this good ending happen?*'

We ran this process once with an experienced woman who was about to make the long-awaited career move from a senior position in a large national consumer goods company to a parallel post in a truly global multinational. Having given in her three months' notice, Estelle wanted to end her career at the British company on a positive note. The four questions helped her formulate an ending that was right for her and meant she left behind a positive legacy and an excellent professional reputation.

First of all, she decided that a good ending would mean she would have done all she could in her job and set the tone for the future of her department. Secondly, she realised that to do this she would want to leave on a high note, with a successful campaign that proved her marketing strategy for her product group was on the right track. Thirdly, she could see herself making the board-level presentation, unveiling the bright, colourful storyboards, feeling confident and outlining a clear, convincing rationale. When she imagined the scene, she could see the key people nodding, looking engaged, asking perceptive questions and sounding highly enthusiastic. Fourthly, she recognised that achieving this would require her to enlist the active co-operation of her whole department and several outside suppliers to produce exceptional results within a three-month span. Far from the demob-happy cynic some people might have expected, Estelle became very determined and focused on her final project for her last few weeks.

She took the task of creating the right ending very seriously, for herself. But its wider importance was emphasised a few months later when she met her old managing director, more or less on an equal footing now, at a European business conference.

'I don't think we knew what we were losing until after you'd gone,' he said. 'But if you ever want to come back to us, just pick up the phone. And, Estelle, next time we'll make sure you're up there, in the right position.'

It's that 'That's that' feeling

Without proper endings, life becomes a great deal less comfortable. We have a deep need for closure, for the feeling that something can be ticked off and marked down as over, finished and dealt with. There is great satisfaction, even in little things, in knowing that a task or a problem does not have to occupy any more space in our attention or our memory. Lack of closure, however, can make everything much more stressful. Uncompleted tasks and unfinished business impose demands on you, dragging you to and fro from one issue to another and making it cumulatively harder to get anything properly sorted out. Achieving a sense of completion, even about small things, in day-to-day life can make a real contribution to your morale and energy levels. Even the tiniest completions can make a difference to how you feel.

This may well be one of the reasons for the popularity of e-mail. People can jot their thoughts down quickly in an e-mail, with a minimum of fuss and formality, which is attractive in itself. But the fact that the message can then be sent off instantly, at the touch of a button, with no need for a stamp or an envelope and no need to move from your desk, makes it doubly attractive. Within a matter of seconds, everything that needs to be done is done. Press 'send' and it's away. The task is done – at least for now, until the next reply.

There are limits to how much people can deal with at once in their lives, at home or at work. If you do not recognise the need to clear the decks, you will pay a price for this. It is like having too many telephones ringing at once, and too many calls on hold. It is like trying to watch a bank of televisions, each showing a different channel. And it can quickly reduce you to a state of fretful distraction.

Equally stressful is the change that seems to take forever to complete. The stress that goes with buying or selling a house or flat under English property law is a case in point. This is a process that few who have been through it ever forget. For weeks, and often months, you proceed through offers, searches, surveys, negotiations and draft contracts, endlessly thinking you're there, always incurring costs and knowing the deal could evaporate at any moment and continually frustrated in achieving closure, before you finally get to the point where you can say 'It is done'.

On the other hand, quite apart from practical considerations, good endings make you feel good. There are a lot of things you can complete relatively easily as you go through life – and you will usually feel a lot better if you take the opportunity to polish them off while you can.

Tidying up the loose ends

Unfinished business clutters up your brain, your desk and your life. Unpaid bills, unreturned library books, unanswered messages and untended relationships all conspire to put you under pressure. But you can dramatically increase your sense of being in control of your life if you choose to manage it so that there are fewer loose ends in it. By all means get rid of them all, if you have the time, the energy and the motivation to do it. If not, use the following loose ends technique to make a significant start straight away.

Loose Ends Technique

1. Make a list of six of your loose ends.
2. For each bit of unfinished business, check how much better you would feel if this loose end were tidied up and completed.
3. For each item, decide what you will need to do to achieve this.
4. Pick your top three and imagine how different you will feel when all three are done.
5. Decide how you will take action to deal with them in the next forty-eight hours.

Typically, your top three loose ends will include tasks that involve making arrangements with other people. With James it meant organising a meeting, arranging to have the car serviced and fixing up a visit to the dentist. These all tend to mean fiddling around with diaries and juggling your commitments and other people's to make everything fit together. That's why James had been putting them off. But once he'd tasted how different he'd feel if these changes were done, he had the motivation to get moving and pick up the phone. Ten minutes later James felt a lot more in control – even though the dentist couldn't see him for another three weeks.

While most people could benefit from this kind of purposeful approach to the loose ends in their home and personal lives, it is probably not so obvious that many highly competent executives grapple with comparable problems at work. For example, we have recently seen our first serious case of e-mail overwhelm. The victim was Stefan, a senior manager in a multinational corporation, who was receiving so many e-mails every day that he just did not have time to read through them all. He could have spent all day processing e-mails and responding to his incoming messages but the reality was unanswered messages. These piled up, causing real operational problems and leading him to begin to doubt his own competence in the job. At one point he was going home late, then staying up from 11 p.m. to 2 a.m. just trying to catch up with e-mails.

Instead of letting this situation continue and undermine his health and his self-confidence, we suggested, as a matter of urgency, that he should give one of his people the specific task of acting as his e-mail gatekeeper. The effect of introducing this gatekeeper function was almost miraculous. With someone else vetting his messages and only passing on those which absolutely demanded his personal attention, Stefan was freed from what had become an almost intolerable burden, largely caused by the ease with which the sender of an e-mail can copy it to a long list of recipients.

You can apply the same sort of thinking to regain control and reduce your discomfort when your own to-do list threatens to get out of hand. Instead of being driven entirely by the list of unfinished business and the more or less pressing obligations it embodies, it is important to retake the initiative and manage the situation yourself, remembering that every item you can complete on and remove from the list will reduce your stress level.

If you don't choose to take control, you will probably just wait until one thing or another rises to the very top of the to-do list – to the point where putting off tackling it becomes even more of a hassle than doing it. But there is another way.

Start paying attention to how uncomfortable each item on your list makes you feel. Pick out whatever makes you feel most uncomfortable. Know that anything you do that enables you to get closure on this – or even to move towards it – will have a disproportionately beneficial effect on how you feel inside. This in turn will make you much more resourceful.

In NLP we talk about the kinesthetics of an experience, by which we mean the physical sensations you experience when thinking of it or dealing with it. Checking these out gives you a lot of information and also gives rise to the name of this process: 'The "K" Check':

The 'K' Check:
1. Carry out a quick stocktake to identify which items on your to-do list are causing you most discomfort.
2. Pick the one that makes you feel most uncomfortable, but also a few 'quick wins', i.e. things that would be quite quick and easy to do. (If these are one and the same – wonderful!)
3. Consider what you can do to complete – or move towards completion – with this key item.
4. Begin – and while you're at it do the quickies too.

The idea of quick wins is important. These are the tasks that really can be knocked off very quickly, at no great cost in time and effort. They can be removed from your to-do list, once and for all, if only you decide to do them now.

If you intend to pay your bills and the money's there to meet your cheques, do it now. Get those bills out of your life. If you know you ought to phone your mother before the weekend, make the call now. Do the easy things that will make life simpler – and do them without hesitation. In getting rid of them, you will clear the decks and streamline your remaining to-do list, reducing the pressure of your obligations. But you will also get, with each completed job, the positive kick that comes with achieving closure and a corresponding upsurge in your energy, optimism and enthusiasm for life.

As always, we are talking about the essential distinction between running your life and letting it run you. Though the tasks involved may be anything from the trivial to the monumental, it is your approach that makes all the difference.

From closure to congruence

Congruence – the feeling of being all of a piece, without internal conflicts and inconsistencies – is a highly desirable state that often depends on recognising and taking action to deal with various loose ends inside yourself. It is one of the most powerful ideas in NLP, because the difference between a person acting with congruence and a person who is at sixes and sevens with life is something most of us can instinctively recognise and respond to. Congruence breeds clarity in yourself. It makes it possible for ordinary people to utilise the full range of their resources, convince others and achieve extraordinary things. But it is not always easy to feel this wholehearted commitment to what you are doing. There can sometimes be many different aspects of you, different times of your life and different ages of you all contending for your attention and influencing your behaviour. Some of these may no longer be appropriate to the person you are now, in which case some sort of closure is required, so that the old can be done with.

You can do a certain amount of this yourself, if you learn to recognise the little qualms and hesitations inside you that can often draw your attention to an internal contradiction. If you can locate such issues, you may be able to acknowledge their existence, recognise their origins and resolve them yourself to achieve closure. But often, especially with bigger internal conflicts, it's just easier to make these changes with the help of a counsellor or therapist.

Getting closure does not mean 'That's done and I'll never think of it again'. It does mean that this particular strand is no longer a loose thread. It is properly woven into the fabric of your life and taking its appropriate place there. Congruence is about unifying all the different threads that make up the stuff of your personality, so that you can operate effectively, as one whole and integrated individual.

The pay-offs of achieving congruence are well worth the effort. Congruent people can be fast and flexible, moving in any direction at short notice without the drag-anchor of unresolved doubts and contradictions to slow them down. You can feel more comfortable in yourself and vastly more dynamic, decisive and purposeful if you don't have loose ends and competing internal claims to worry about.

If you can't say goodbye, you can't say hello

We know someone whose mother refused to throw anything away – magazines, newspapers, envelopes, even boxes and cartons. Her house steadily filled up with these things until it became physically impossible to live a normal life there. On opening the front door, you realised it was partly blocked by piles of old newspapers and that these extended into a room that was full, from floor to ceiling, of old magazines, colour supplements, paper bags and twenty years' worth of junk mail. A narrow passageway was all that remained of what had once been a living room. It was an extraordinary sight. It felt weird – and it got worse when you realised that the whole house was like this. This was the home of a woman who had lost the ability to let go.

But what about the mental or emotional equivalent of this? Ask yourself this question, 'Have I got room in my life to live properly?' It's a serious question. For the thwarted lover who spends years fantasising about someone who is long gone from his life, the answer is no. While this pining continues, there is no space available for a new relationship. There is often a need to close off, before the heart can open again.

In business, too, there often needs to be an ending to make way for the beginning of a new phase in a company's growth. The small, friendly start-up firm, running on enthusiasm, long hours and the personal commitment and stamina of the original staff, may need to say goodbye to this ethos if it is to grow beyond a certain point. As it is reborn, with less dependence on the personalities and skills of a few key people, and more reliance on systems and roles, working practices will change and people may feel that something special risks being lost. This is often a difficult adjustment for the founders of a business to make. But it can be a fatal mistake to try to cling on to the old, familiar ways.

Since this need for an appropriate ending is important in so many personal and business contexts, it is worth stopping for a moment and checking your own circumstances. Ask yourself whether there is an ending you need that you have not, perhaps, acknowledged. You can take stock now. Ask yourself the following questions:

1. 'What now needs to be in the past?'
2. 'Am I preventing myself from getting more of what I want because I haven't let go?'

In our business skills training, it is not at all uncommon for someone to find that looking at his or her business through this prism throws a completely new light on current problems. In more personal matters, using this can often highlight barriers of inertia or obstinacy that keep friends or family members apart for years after an original slight or misunderstanding has lost its significance. Rock fans will recognise the classic scenario of the Mike and the Mechanics hit, 'The Living Years', in which a man laments failing to make his peace with his father before the old man dies. It's a story that is played out in different forms in many families. The feelings of remorse, guilt and incompleteness mean that the survivor can suffer for a very long time from this lack of closure.

How well you round things off and take your leave of them is often a lot more important than it seems at the time. It is well worth thinking in terms of spring-cleaning your life from time to time, to make sure that everything you carry forward with you is of some use to you. It may be time to say goodbye to old, limiting beliefs that have held you back. These may be beliefs about your own capabilities and potential, about what you deserve in life, about what is possible and what is not or about any number of other issues that shape and colour your approach to living. If you're ready to take action to deal with this kind of hangover from the past, it will probably be worth finding an experienced NLP counsellor or therapist to help you do it. The techniques and processes certainly exist in NLP, and this is one area where it is especially valuable to work with the help and guidance of another person.

PART III

To Manage is to Live

Chapter 8

Your Health

The first wealth is health.
Ralph Waldo Emerson

It's a whole life policy

It's easy to give glib advice to people who want to improve their health: if you're young, take up a sport; if you're not, take up exercise of some sort; if you're old, get a dog.

But what do we really mean when we talk about being healthy? It's pretty obvious that health means more than just the absence of disease, even if many of us fall into the trap of taking our health very much for granted until we are deprived of it.

If someone has been ill, of course, the contrast between sickness and normality may prompt us to comment. But in day-to-day life, the only time it ever spontaneously occurs to us to register that someone appears healthy is if this person also looks happy. It's hard to imagine the two being separated. 'He looks angry and upset, but very healthy' just sounds odd. For most of us, our perception of health is almost always tied in with some notion of being relaxed and cheerful, with positive behaviour, a lack of anxiety and an abundance of energy. This is interesting, because it shows how we instinctively mix mental and physical factors together. Most people have a surprisingly broad and holistic idea of what being healthy really means. It's a view that's justified by history, too, as the word 'health' derives originally from the idea of wholeness. In NLP, where the interaction between your body and your mind is recognised as the starting point for many practical life-management techniques, the idea that health is more than just physical and mechanical is very important.

People who take a methodical, systematic approach to their lives and their careers often have a problem sorting out their attitudes to health. Wealth is easy. You can work at it, build it up, bank it and rely on it to be there for you when you need it at a later date. Health is different. Because people think you can't store it up for later, they treat it like the weather – as something that happens to you and that you cannot begin to influence. Yet we know this is not true. You can decide to start doing exercise or taking the dog for a walk twice a day, come rain or shine, and know that the change will influence your health for the better. You can never take total control over your health, but you can go a long way towards determining what happens to you.

How are you getting on?

In training people how to manage their lives, we have found that it often helps them to go through a short personal health audit – though this is very different from the physical screening programmes run by hospitals and health clinics. For one thing, the answers are all subjective reactions that cannot be measured with the usual machines. What's more, just focusing on the questions set out below will immediately take you some way towards improving the way you live and the way you treat yourself. The basic questions will only take you a few minutes to answer, but we suggest that you will get a lot more out of the exercise if you do this with paper and pencil and note down your answers, so that you can refer back to them later.

The Health Audit
1. How healthy are you now? (Rate yourself on a scale of 1–100)
2. If you continue with your present lifestyle, how healthy do you expect to be in twenty years' time? (Scale 1–100)
3. What could make you more healthy?
4. What can you identify in your life now that contributes to your health and sense of well-being?
5. What could you be doing to get more of this?
6. What is there in your life now that detracts from your health and sense of well-being?
7. What could you do to ensure that there was less of this negative influence in your life?
8. Do you need an alarm clock to wake you up each morning?
9. How good is the quality of your sleep?
10. Do you suffer from constant time pressure, as if you are always a bit behind?

There are many other factors that affect your health and well-being, and we will investigate some more of them later. For now, though, let's look at your ten answers and see what can be learned from them.

How healthy are you now?

The first six questions, starting off from your own subjective assessment of where you are now and your guess at where you expect to be in twenty years' time, are unusual, because they ask you to assess the situation yourself, rather than hand over responsibility to a doctor or other professional. One of the problems with health is that some people feel their well-being is hardly even their own business – it's almost as if it belongs to the medical profession and not to the individual concerned. By making your own broad, overall assessment of the present state of play and the likely outlook a couple of decades ahead, you begin to focus on the links between how you choose to live and how your body is likely to respond over the medium to long term. Already, by the time you arrive at the third question ('What could make you more healthy?'), you will be noticing that there are many possible answers.

If you smoke, or take drugs, or recognise that you are far too fond of alcohol, modifying your habits is obviously going to make a difference – and you don't need anyone to give you a lecture about how vital it is to put yourself back in control. If you simply lead a dull, sedentary lifestyle, you already know that getting up and doing something to make your heart beat faster will have all kinds of positive pay-offs. If you eat too much, sleep too little, drive too fast, hate your job, wish away your time, argue with your family, work ridiculous hours, worry about everything or dislike yourself, it's just as important to make a change. None of this is doing you any good at all now – and it's certainly not setting you up to be in good shape in twenty years' time.

Just thinking about what could make you more healthy, in relation to the particular things that drag you down and make you feel under par, can be a liberating experience. Most of us have a lot more resources and understanding inside ourselves than we are in the habit of using or revealing. Most of us know what we really need, even if we are sometimes reluctant to admit it. And even if we don't already know all the answers, thinking constructively about this question is a good start.

Question 4 ('What can you identify in your life now that contributes to your health and sense of well-being?') and the follow-up Q5 ('What could you be doing to get more of this?') offer another way of getting at the same thing. If you can put your finger on what makes a positive contribution to your life now, you stand a good chance of recognising how you can get more. It sounds too simple for words. But, of course, that is by no means the way most of us live our daily lives.

When Sandy realised that commuting by car through heavy traffic every day meant she was habitually tense and tired before she even started work, she decided this was not doing her any good. She was suffering from recurrent headaches and repeated bouts of flu and had even considered quitting her job. But she seized on our suggestion that she should change her route to work for a longer, but less urban, drive that took her on a looping course through woods and open countryside before bringing her into the town centre. The result has been entirely positive. Sandy gets off to a better start each day. Even though she drives further, the journey is often slightly quicker, because of the lack of congestion. 'Every day I see deer grazing,' she said. 'It makes a big difference.' She is happier in her job and the headaches have gone.

Once you decide to take a broad view of what health and well-being are about, you realise, for example, that being happy is good for you. Simply doing something you enjoy and that puts you in a positive frame of mind is good for your health. A daily routine that was planned around this principle would be unrecognisable to most people. But it may be much easier than you think. Start with the little things because they're not so little.

Don't let it get you down

If being happy makes us healthy, it's also true that being unhappy is bad for our health. There is plenty of medical evidence of the mechanisms that link your state of mind to the way your glands, your hormones and your immune system operate. If you are down in the dumps, you are weakened at every level. You are more likely to catch whatever bugs are going round. You are more likely to make mistakes or be involved in an accident. Your social skills are suppressed, making it less likely that people will be attracted to spend time with you and this automatically increases your sense of isolation. Your energy level is low. You feel more tired, think less clearly and have fewer ideas. Your judgement is impaired, about situations, people and yourself. All in all, you are diminished as a person.

No one goes through life without the occasional dip into these darker regions. But one of the marks of someone who is managing his or her life is the way this person uses a range of simple techniques to take positive action and reclaim control of the situation when the shadows come crowding in. Focusing on what makes you happy and taking immediate steps to get more of it is one of the fundamental principles of this approach. Another approach is implied in Q6, 'What is there in your life now that detracts from your health and sense of well-being?' and the follow-up to that 'What could you do to ensure that there was less of this negative influence in your life?'.

Most people don't have to pause long to think about what gets on their nerves, at work, at home or travelling between the two. Routine niggles are often the worst, because things that annoy you at about the same time every day become embedded in your expectation of the day and can start to irritate before you have even got to them. Examples of this sort of irritant are the totally predictable boss who taps his watch meaningfully every time you walk in one minute late or the children who switch straight into sulks and whining the moment a parent mentions bedtime. But the negative influences that diminish your sense of well-being may not be all in the mind. We met a young man recently who was beginning to think there was something very wrong with his health. Despite examinations and fruitless investigations by his doctor, Andrew was suffering from unexplained stomach pains that were leaving him wearied, debilitated and a prey to all kinds of nameless fears. Yet the solution to his health problem was such a seemingly trivial thing. 'You're wearing a belt,' said Ian McDermott. 'Is it too tight? Try opening it up a notch for a couple of days and let me know if that makes a difference.' The call came three days later. 'I can't believe it. That's amazing,' said Andrew. 'The problem's gone and I feel a hundred times better in myself.' Sometimes the simple solution that's needed may be staring you in the face. But if you approach it with too many assumptions in place, you can search for the answer in vain.

The art of ring-fencing

Health issues are not always obviously about health. Your well-being can be undermined just as effectively by nagging doubts and anxieties as it can by illness. The big worry areas – financial, legal, educational and family – can obviously put people under acute pressure at times. Yet often, when we know nothing can be done to solve a problem, at least in the short term, it is possible to ring-fence the issue so that it does not overshadow too much of your day-to-day life.

Some people live, for example, balancing mountains of debt. If you ask why the overdraft is not cleared or the other debts paid off, you will often find that scratching the surface reveals a very worried person. But there is usually constructive action you can take. The secret is to bring the situation under your control by negotiating a way forward with the lender, even if this means paying off very small amounts over a long period. This way, the lender knows what's going on and you know an agreement regarding repayment is in place. As long as you fulfil your part of the new bargain, the issue is dealt with. In a situation like this, you may wish the debt didn't exist, but once it is ring-fenced and contained and not seeping into other areas of your life, you can breathe more freely and feel lighter.

We helped Gerald make use of this approach after his small printing company went down, leaving him with massive debts. His testimony is typical and you can even hear clues about how important it was to his health, in the very physical way he talks about the situation. 'It made a huge difference – facing this and finding it was only part of my life,' he says. 'It meant I could reclaim my life, rather than having the problems infect everything. I knew it would take a long time to sort the mess out, but now there's a plan and it's agreed, I can breathe a sigh of relief. I can get on with my life, because now it's mine again.'

By looking at what there is in your daily existence that detracts from your health and well-being and thinking about ways to eliminate, reduce or ring-fence these factors, you can achieve surprisingly significant results.

Perhaps the most powerfully negative factors of all, in terms of their effect on people's health and morale, are relationship problems, in or outside the family. Notice that Q7 'What could you do to ensure that there was less of this negative influence in your life?' asks what you yourself could do. It might be wonderful if someone else had a spontaneous change of attitude, but you can't spend your life waiting for this to happen. Your mind needs to be scanning all the possibilities for you to take the initiative and make the changes that will give you 'less of this negative influence' in your life.

Again, the principle of ring-fencing can be utilised to your advantage. The very first move towards making an infuriating work colleague less of a trial is to ensure that you do not spend your time at home thinking about him or her and the incidents that have upset you during the day. By all means unload and get things off your chest when you first come in. Then stop. Do something different. Resist the temptation to relive again and again the dramas of the working day on the home stage.

In a way, though, it is often easier to let go of irritations and conflicts at work because you can, literally, leave them behind. The environment and context in which such problems loom so large and seem so important can sometimes be switched off as you return home, forcing a healthy change of perspective. But this is not so true of relationship problems within the home. These are played out on an immovable stage. When that happens, instead of being a retreat, home becomes a place of conflict and tension, inseparable from the routines of daily life. It takes intuitive skill or learned technique to avoid the tendency to escalation that can accompany even minor conflicts in the home.

One way to bring the build-ups of tension under control is to bring them out into the open. Instead of the mind-reading and second-guessing that so often lead to friction and misunderstanding in close relationships, it is often possible to lay down rules of engagement, in a calm moment, that will benefit everyone when the temperature starts to rise. If you can agree a rule, for example, that both parties should state their feelings, rather than bottling them up, this will usually be a good start.

If you can also agree that people should take ultimate responsibility for their own reactions, you have made another step forward. 'I'm feeling angry and unwanted' is a lot better than a silent and smouldering resentment. 'You've come in late and I'm feeling angry and unwanted' is even better, because it indicates a supposed sequence of action and reaction, but doesn't make the claim that the one thing is entirely and directly a result of the other. Just employing the word 'and' to link the two halves of this sort of sentence is very useful. It allows you to say things that would be a lot more attacking and provocative if they were expressed as cause and effect, using words like 'because'.

There is no doubt that the state of your most intimate relationships, with lovers, friends and family, is a major influence on your own well-being and your physical, as well as psychological, health. But it cuts both ways. Paying due attention to the physical side of your life will also play a big part in determining how you feel about everything that goes on around you – including the people in your life.

How is your recovery time?

When it comes to talking about your physical health, the first problem is often one of definition and terminology. What do we mean by health? Is it the same as fitness? Does it depend on what you do or don't do – or what you eat or don't eat? What does health mean at different ages and stages of life?

Many of us actually carry round with us a whole ragbag of inconsistent and even contradictory beliefs and ideas about the subject. We are confused by the information we get from the media and perplexed by the everyday paradoxes we observe. Is the person in the aerobics class who has a cold healthy or unhealthy? And why is it that professional athletes and sports stars seem so prone to physical deterioration, once they retire?

Somewhere, embedded in this confusion, is the sensible notion that health is something that can exist independent of occasional coughs and colds. The fact that someone has picked up some minor seasonal ailment does not necessarily tell you anything about that person's overall state of health. Good health makes you more resistant to passing bugs, but it does not make you immune to new viruses or old-fashioned bacteria. Sometimes you will be more susceptible than others and you will crawl off to bed, feeling like death warmed up. When this happens, one of the benefits of underlying good health is a noticeably shorter recovery time before you are back on your feet again.

Athletes in training place a good deal of emphasis, these days, on recovery time as an index of overall health and fitness. By keeping track of the time an athlete's heart rate takes to return to normal after peak exertion, it is possible to chart the beneficial effects of a rigorous training programme. As the recovery time that is needed gets shorter, what was a stretch becomes something the athlete can take in his or her stride and targets can be pushed to higher and higher levels without undue risk of injury. For the rest of us, the length of time we take to recover after clambering up a slope, carrying a heavy object or running for a train is just as much an indicator of our overall fitness.

But recovery time is not just physical. How well you are able to handle the emotional and psychological demands that arise in your life is equally significant. It's not that if you are in good overall health nothing gets to you. No one is immune to shocks and surprises. But what is important is how rapidly you are able to regain your balance and equilibrium.

You've got to start somewhere

You don't need a book like this to tell you what you need to do to improve your health. You know many of the answers yourself already, though you may be interested to ask yourself why you don't put what you know into practice in this area as much as you could. Many people have an unacknowledged feeling that they are going to fall so far short of the ideal that it is not worth bothering. This is nonsense – and dangerous nonsense, too. To see just how easily you could be improving your overall health and your general quality of life, set yourself the task of jotting down five answers to the following question:

What could I do to build up my health?

1. ....

2. ....

3. ....

4. ....

5. ....

The answers you have suggested here may be quite predictable. For many people, they will be to do with simple changes like taking more exercise, eating more wisely, getting more sleep, giving up bad habits and thinking more positively. People know they would feel better and be stronger, more resilient and probably happier if they did these things, but often they still don't do them. The secret is to understand that putting into practice even one of the changes you listed when you answered the question above will be an improvement. Two will make a real difference, three a transformation.

One change implemented is worth more than any number of books read or good intentions. So here's one way to make it easy to start. Pick one of your changes and give yourself just a taste of it. See if it makes any difference to how you feel and notice if it has any other good spin-offs.

Jim was a 3-stone-overweight manager who once upon a time had been super fit and played squash to win five times a wcck. But that had been ten years ago. On his form, in answer to the question, 'What could I do to build up my health?', he'd written 'Start running'. But he had also said he felt like he couldn't think clearly. He was afraid he would not be promoted at work because he wasn't really being creative or contributing anything original.

After we'd talked he knew he wanted some of that old vitality back again. When he got home he went for a brisk ten-minute walk. He was shocked to find he was out of breath. But he did it again the next day. A couple of days went by, then he did it again and it was easier. Now he goes for short, easy runs. 'It's so different not having to go all out,' he said. 'I think I'm enjoying my mini-runs more than I ever did the squash. I don't understand why but I'm feeling more alert and confident at work. Suddenly I feel motivated.'

Your body is surprisingly malleable and responsive in adapting to even minor changes in your routine, so you'll notice pay-offs much sooner than you expect. (Additional exercise techniques can be found in the tape set *NLP: Health and Well-being* by McDermott and O'Connor, Thorsons Audio.) You can do more than you think, more quickly than you think. But you do have to make a start, or nothing will happen.

An investment in balance

However carefully you attend to the physical factors, like exercise and diet, being truly healthy demands more than the smooth functioning of a well-maintained machine.

If your life is unbalanced, there is a serious danger that it will also be unhealthy. If you are super-successful, but so driven that you never get the chance to spend time doing nothing, to laugh with your friends, be with children or play with animals, there is a lack of balance that will eventually catch up with you one way or another.

Wherever there is a lack of balance, there is a risk to your medium to long-term health. Conversely, the more of a real, fluid, dynamic equilibrium you can build into your life, the healthier you are likely to be. It is worth thinking consciously about what activities bring a sense of balance to your life and whether you need to create the opportunity to do more of them, not just for your short-term pleasure, but for your long-term health as well. The investment of time and attention now can be so small that you feel no loss at all. The pay-offs come back to you with compound interest over the years – and the earlier you make a start, the better the returns you are likely to achieve.

Chapter 9

Wealth

It is better to live rich than to die rich.
Samuel Johnson

The man in a hurry

When Joe left college, his first job was selling chocolate bars to newsagents and corner shops. After six years, he moved on, first to insurance and then, at just the right moment, into mobile phones. A good, enthusiastic young salesman could not go wrong in such a market at that time and Joe didn't. After three years of fast cars and huge commissions, he knew just what to do next. He borrowed some cash, opened a shop of his own and advertised deals that undercut everyone in sight to get customers in through the door. 'I was never going to get rich working for someone else,' he said. 'This way, whatever happens – success or failure – it's down to me. But I know what people want and I know there's a lot of money to be made by giving them the right sort of deal. I don't have a target, but I certainly don't aim to be working by the time I'm forty.'

Joe's business grew fast; from one shop to a dozen, with some juicy corporate accounts to back it up, and his personal style became the company's trade mark. He made a point of being visible and he seemed to be everywhere, all the time. Staff and customers got used to the way he always seemed to be there in person, wherever things were happening. His sober but powerful BMW always seemed to be collecting tickets on the yellow lines outside his shops, but, as Joe said, that cost less than wasting time finding somewhere to park near town centre sites.

One damp day, it all went wrong. Joe and the BMW slid into the back of a gravel truck and Joe woke up on a drip, with an earnest young consultant explaining that the internal injuries were not as bad as they had feared and that they would operate that evening in the hope of saving his leg. The operation was successful, but it was days before Joe was even in a fit state to see any visitors apart from his wife Helen and the children. As they patched him up and put him back together again, he had plenty of time to think. At first, he kept calling the office, fretting about uncompleted deals and worrying about how his team would manage. But soon a strange feeling came over him. One morning, he woke up and realised that he was enjoying being in hospital far too much.

It was a watershed in Joe's life. He had been growing the business and making money hand over fist for several years, but he suddenly realised that he had had no time to enjoy the fortune that was piling up. His children were growing up spending very little time in his company and he hadn't even known the younger daughter was learning the flute until she passed her Grade 1 exam. He had been going to bed late and sleeping badly for months before the crash. And his relationship with Helen had been, well, more functional than enthusiastic. 'What have I been doing?' he thought. 'I used to enjoy this business. I used to enjoy my life. Now just being stuck in hospital seems like a bonus, because it's forcing me to take a break.'

What does wealth cost?

For Joe, a couple of years past forty, sole owner of a thriving mobile phone company, as rich as anyone could ever need to be and suddenly given an unasked-for chance to review his life, the big questions were looming. What was he going to do for the next fifteen or twenty years? If he was going to work, what was it all for? What was the purpose of the wealth he had accumulated? And where did relationships fit into his list of priorities?

Joe was bold. He picked the brightest and most committed of his young managers, told him that he would make him rich if he earned it and set him to run the day-to-day business of the company. Joe restricted himself to two to three days a week, setting up new deals, making the strategic decisions and nursing the relationships with major customers. He spent more time with the family, took up gliding and made sure that he, or he and Helen, got away for some sort of break every five or six weeks. He also started spending some of the money on buying grandfather clocks, until he ran out of rooms to put them in.

In fact, after the turning point of the crash, Joe took the hint and did all the things the experts currently recommend, apart, perhaps, from taking up some more active physical activity and losing a little weight. He reassessed his life, marshalled his assets and priorities and had a major rethink. He also arrived, entirely of his own accord, at the belief that maybe even his accident wasn't entirely accidental. Whether it was a providential warning for him or a direct result of the constant stress and tiredness in his life didn't seem to matter. What mattered was that it brought about a major change.

Wealth doesn't usually come free. If you've got money, but you have achieved this at the cost of your marriage, your health, relationships with friends and your personal integrity, there is an obvious question that needs to be asked. What is the cost of your wealth?

If nothing else, you will have had to pay the opportunity cost of your wealth, the cost of all the alternative opportunities that you have not been able to take up because your time and attention were already spoken for. Every choice you make rules out some other options. So if you are going to give up a lot, it had better be worth it. And if you take the decision to go all out for wealth, the next question that arises is equally blunt. What do you want it for?

Here is a revealing exercise that you should do right now, before reading on any further. We have used it in many business and NLP training situations and the results never fail to surprise people. Find a pen and set aside just a minute or two to fill in ten slots in answer to the question below.

And this question is 'What are the ten things that having wealth would give you?' Your answers can be as brief as you like, in any sort of shorthand that will make sense to you when you come back to them later.

The top ten things wealth would give me:

1. ....

2. ....

3. ....

4. ....

5. ....

6. ....

7. ....

8. ....

9. ....

10. ....

The significance of doing this as a written exercise, rather than just asking you to think about what wealth could do for you, will become apparent very soon. If you have written in your answers, we can now compare them with the sort of lists that other people come up with. Let's look first at a list, produced by someone who already has most of what he feels he needs in life and whose idea of wealth is pretty down to earth and materialistic:

The top ten things wealth could give me:
1. A larger house.
2. A better car.
3. Holidays abroad.
4. Interesting clothes.
5. Meals in top restaurants.
6. A boat.
7. A holiday home.
8. Fine wines.
9. Flights on Concorde.
10. Presents for friends and family.

No great surprises here, are there? This is similar to the kind of generic wish list that goes with imagining winning the lottery. Compare it with the list set out below:

The top ten things wealth would give me:
1. Independence.

2. Security.
3. A larger house.
4. I'd be able to leave my job.
5. Time (to relax and enjoy things).
6. —
7. —
8. —
9. —
10. —

This person, whose selection of ten items tailed off after five, clearly has a completely different approach to the idea of wealth. It is seen, first of all, as a means of escape from what is obviously a less-than-satisfactory lifestyle.

It suggests that he is doomed to feel insecure and pressured and to stay in a job that he does not like because he is not wealthy. In some rare and extreme cases, that might be true. But there are not many people who really have so few options in their lives that they are condemned to bear all these burdens unless they can achieve wealth. Lack of time to relax and feelings of insecurity, for example, are as likely to be to do with ineffective life management as with purely economic pressures.

The contrast between this person's list and the previous one is interesting. The man who made the first list, and who clearly had no difficulty filling all ten slots, was showing a fairly normal, unambitious, unimaginative approach to the idea of wealth. The items he listed were all, more or less, 'just out of reach' things – better versions of the clothes, holidays, cars and meals he already enjoyed. The boat and the holiday home were slightly different attempts to gear up and think what a very different level of spending power might make possible. But there were no executive jets or private islands, no palaces and no ambitions to fulfil dreams by mounting expeditions to the North Pole, founding an opera company or buying Chelsea Football Club or the Miami Dolphins.

The original question, 'What do you want it for?', takes on a different slant when you compare these very different attitudes to the idea of wealth. It is a well-worn cliché that money can't buy you happiness. But if it does offer the harassed compiler of the second list the opportunity to leave his irksome job and do something else with his life, it will certainly be making a contribution towards his happiness.

Money can't buy me ... what?

It is easy to get mealy-mouthed about what money can and can't buy. NLP certainly has no bias against the making and enjoyment of money. But because it equips individuals to know, with unusual clarity, what their real wants in life are, it is relentless in its insistence that money is no good to people unless they understand how to use it. A key part of the art of using wealth, for example, is finding ways to make practical things that you can buy deliver you the big abstract benefits (like independence, security or time to relax) that you need.

No one can buy time. But there are occasions when paying for a taxi will give you the option to use a few minutes for what you want to do, rather than spending that time walking or using public transport. Money can't buy you love. But it can, directly, buy you a sexual experience, if that is what you want. And it can be used to buy presents and flowers and finance outings, meals and a host of other activities that will indirectly enhance the prospects of love finding a foothold. Indeed, the very presence of wealth can be conducive to love. Every reader of Jane Austen will remember that touching moment in *Pride and Prejudice* when the incorruptible Elizabeth Bennet first sets eyes on Pemberley,

Darcy's magnificent country house in Derbyshire, and suddenly realises how badly she may have misjudged the man.

So what are the real, practical limits? When it comes to it, very few indeed. Wealth generally gets a pretty poor press, when you consider how much most of us desire it. You may need imagination, ingenuity and resourcefulness to find ways of translating your wealth into those great abstract goals you want in your life, but you would certainly need them anyway if you were going for the same goals without the leverage of wealth to help you on your way. Other things being equal, having wealth gives you a lot more options than not having it. And that means that, as long as you keep an eye on the price you are paying and you don't let it get too high, aiming to build up a certain amount of personal wealth is a constructive part of almost any realistic life-management programme.

What does your idea of wealth add up to?

If you start asking people what their idea of wealth is, you invariably trigger some interesting and unexpected responses. So what is wealth for you? A hundred thousand? A million? If you made a million, would you feel wealthy? Is that pounds, or could it be dollars or German marks? There seems to be something absolute and unassailable about having a million, as if once you have that no one's ever going to be able to take it all away from you again. The theory obviously needs modifying when you come to think in terms of currencies like the peseta, the drachma or lire and roubles, but the concept of millionairedom still hasn't been eroded by inflation, in Britain or even the US, despite the huge fall in the value of a million since the word 'millionaire' was coined, in the 1820s.

Even if we agree to settle for a million as a rough and ready definition of wealth, does that tell us everything we need to know about the subject? It doesn't, because there is also the idea that wealth has some sort of depth and permanence about it. You can have money, then spend it or lose it and be left with nothing. When we talk about wealth, it's different. The idea of wealth implies an ability to renew itself, like the wealth Joe derived from his mobile phone empire. However much he spent, the vitality of Joe's business ensured that the coffers would be replenished and his wealth would be restored. In the same way, people who have highly valued talents in themselves or whose wealth is consolidated into large amounts of property, which can never lose more than a proportion of its value, know that they have wealth they can't be parted from.

To the outsider, this type of unchallengeable wealth looks like a large part of the recipe for a genuinely comfortable life. Yet one of the ironies that makes wealth such a fascinating subject is that many wealthy people are simply not happy. They may be tense and ill at ease with others. They may be prickly or paranoid and find it hard to form relationships. They may be so full of themselves they can empty a room in seconds.

Anyone for a bargain?

It is quite common to find people who have worked so hard to acquire wealth that they can't find the brake pedal and slow down now that they have achieved their goals. Or they may have done so little to deserve their wealth that they live with a permanent feeling that they are frauds and that some divine retribution will descend on them and snatch it away. Some we have known have been so keen not to let their wealth slip away that they have lived lives where they were asset rich but cash poor, scratching and scraping around to find bargains all the time and making it a rule of life never to pay the full price for anything. These are the people with beautiful homes and huge mortgages who tell you how difficult it is to make ends meet and who even want you to sympathise.

It is interesting to consider the mentality of bargain-hunting. Are you getting something for nothing? No. Usually the best you can do is get more for less. Too often, though, it is just more of what you don't particularly want. So would you rather have more of what you don't really want at a knockdown price? Or would you be willing to pay the full price for what you really want?

The millionaire bargain-hunter, like so many other people, can end up with a freezer full of inedible food and a wardrobe full of bargains that he or she seldom wants to wear. These are the consequences of a poverty mentality – items that are expensive at any price, because they do not satisfy your needs. Have you ever thought about costing all your clothes to see which items have really given you the best value, in terms of price divided by the number of wearings you have had out of them? It's an interesting exercise. Like most people, you are almost sure to find that some of your most expensive clothes, looked at this way, are the ones you bought as bargains.

What's been stopping you so far?

The only question that really matters about wealth, for 95 per cent of the population, is 'How do I get it?'

The first step, as always, is know what you want. Make sure you have been through all the NLP techniques we have explained earlier to help you refine and focus on the goals that you set for yourself. Knowing what you want and what specific form success must take to spur you on and draw you towards it is an immensely powerful motivator.

At the same time, there may be real obstacles within you that need to be tackled, if you are ever going to fulfil your potential. The people who do achieve wealth are not necessarily the boldest, the cleverest, the most talented, sensitive, hardworking or worthwhile individuals. But they are the people who have nothing inside them pulling in a different direction and compromising their efforts. So ask yourself what may seem a strange question:

'How have I managed to not generate wealth?

Just for a moment, assume that wealth would already have come to you naturally, if you had not somehow stopped it from happening. Make the question more specific. Ask yourself:

'How have I managed to not generate wealth up until now?'

Your answers may surprise you. Certainly, the answers people have given us have been very varied. Some people have concluded that they have been too busy earning a living to make any money and have decided that they should start their own businesses. Other answers have involved recognising important internal barriers. As one man put it, in a startling flash of insight: 'I've just realised – I've never been able to do it, because I've never thought I was worth it'. For some people, it has been a question of hauling themselves to the brink of success and then losing their nerve or even sabotaging their own efforts in a variety of more or less unconscious ways. For others, missing out on wealth has been more a matter of making lots of money, but being unable to hold on to it. But the most common reason of all is people's apparent inability to be clear about what they really want.

So ask yourself what you want this money for? That's what you're really going for – the money is just a means to an end. And if what you're going for starts to come your way before you get the money, make sure that you recognise it, value it and don't squander it in the name of creating wealth.

How am I going to get it?

If you really want to accumulate wealth you are probably going to need to start your own business. We can point you towards several useful approaches that have good track records and high success rates. But most of them depend on developing one particular skill – the knack of recognising what can create wealth. Once you have spotted a business opportunity that has the potential to create wealth for somebody, you can then set about developing that potential to the full and making sure that that somebody is you. Without the ability to recognise what can create wealth, the process cannot even get under way. So start getting curious about people who have achieved what you're aiming at. Get to know their thinking by reading about them and watching how they do what they do.

Three routes to a wealth-creating idea

Some people inherit wealth, some people win it and some people marry into it – but very few. If you do not already have a burning sense of mission and a great idea that you are sure could carry you to a fortune, that is no bar to generating wealth. Most fortunes do not stem from great and original ideas. You do need an idea – but only incurable romantics necessarily believe it has to be all your own work.

As a general rule, it is a lot easier to take the best of other people's ideas than to put yourself under pressure to come up with a brilliantly original idea of your own. We have three serious suggestions we can offer you right now. And the first one, proven time and again, is to go away for a week or two.

1. Take a holiday.

It may be best to book your holiday flight to one of the world's rich and technologically advanced countries, such as the US or Japan, Germany or Norway, but we would not want to be too dogmatic about this. What is important though, is that you go where there are people – your idyllic, I'm-not-moving-off-this-lounger beach holiday will have to wait for another time.

The point of the holiday is to let ideas find you. By being in a different environment, seeing, hearing and feeling different things all day and every day, you gain two separate forms of stimulation. One relates to your own thinking. While you are superficially occupied taking in the sights, the sounds and the experiences of an unfamiliar country, your brain is automatically taken slightly away from its normal concerns and contexts. On holiday, you live in the present, with less thought than usual about what happened yesterday and what is due to happen tomorrow. As a result, there is less clutter inside your head, and a lot more opportunity than usual for your brain to get on with all sorts of unconscious processing, including putting together scraps of disjointed thought and mulling over half-considered ideas. This is a fertile and potentially productive state and you may want to make a real effort to cultivate it while you are abroad.

The second form of stimulation comes from seeing how things are done differently in a different country. Bringing back a successful idea from somewhere else and adapting and exploiting it to suit your home market is a classic entrepreneur's approach. Importing ideas seen overseas is the mechanism that brought us jacuzzis from California, tapas bars from Spain and tamagotchi toys from Japan – all of which have, in their time, created considerable wealth for the people who transplanted the ideas.

More than twenty years ago, a friend of ours was travelling in Thailand and kept admiring the smooth, hand-carved teak bowls he ate from. Working with the families in a remote village, he set up an Anglo-Thai business, on a co-operative basis, to produce teakware and market it, first in Britain and later all over Europe. He made good money, moved on, and the business is now wholly Thai-owned, but his initiative has financed many benefits for the villagers, including a children's health centre. Yet it all stemmed from one person thinking 'That's interesting – I've never seen anything quite like that at home.'

2. Spot a parallel between one industry and another and carry an idea across.

With this one you don't even need to invest in a holiday. If you can take a technique or a procedure that works well in one industry and apply it in another where it has not been used before, you may well have the basis of a genuinely wealth-creating idea. But it's striking how often people miss these extra applications.

For example, our local taxi firm spotted the way mail order retailers and companies that take credit card orders over the phone would often ask for a postcode, followed by the house number. From these, the operator would be able to read off the full address from a computer screen. Reasoning that this would be a good way of confirming addresses when its drivers were called out, especially at night, the cab company investigated the possibilities and its two dispatchers now use a Royal Mail Postcode Address File software package that would more usually be seen in a big call centre. The costs of false callouts and incorrect addresses have been virtually eliminated and the firm has grown rapidly since introducing the new technology.

That's just one car hire firm though. What about all the others across the country who might be willing to buy the software? Here's a business opportunity, perhaps – but not until someone has the vision to make it happen.

So ask yourself if there is any practice or way of doing things you have seen or heard of that can be transposed to another context and which would reduce costs or increase profits. If there is, you might end up like the man who sold a low-price furniture company a very significant cost-cutting idea – only finishing the outside surfaces of its inexpensive, flat-packed fibreboard and chipboard furniture. The idea may or may not have been borrowed from the matchbox companies' practice of putting only one striking strip on each box of matches, instead of two. But wherever it came from, it is said to have been valuable enough for its originator to retire on the proceeds.

3. Do what you really want to do. Do it brilliantly and make it work.

The third way of finding out what you could do to create real wealth is to examine what you have to offer the world. If there is something you are really motivated to do, you should start from the assumption that this is not an idle dream but what you should really be doing.

However great your motivation, though, you can't just pile in. Once you have decided what you want to do, you still need to work out just how you are going to be able to make it pay. Ask yourself:

'How am I going to do what I love doing in such a way that others will benefit – and value the benefits so highly that they'll be pleased to pay me money?'

Like many people you may have some talent in a particular direction that is enjoyable and satisfying at an amateur or hobby level, but just not good enough to form the basis for a career. Nevertheless, if there is something you know about and love doing, it is wrong to assume that you cannot tap into this enthusiasm in some productive way. Someone of thirty-five is probably not suddenly going to emerge as a champion downhill skier or tennis player or Formula 1 racing driver. But knowledge and experience in one of these areas might still have some potential relevance to this person's work or possible career. Insurance firms support many sporting events, newspapers write about them, merchandising companies sell to supporters, and clothing and equipment suppliers use big events as the centrepieces of their marketing. Your sports expertise could therefore be an asset in a career in insurance, journalism or marketing, as well as in many other areas that have more tenuous sporting links.

On the road to a fortune

One example of the Route 3, do-what-you-love approach is the story of Tony Wheeler, whose passion and curiosity for travelling in strange places on low budgets led to the birth of one of the world's best-known travel publishing companies, Lonely Planet.

In the early 1970s, Wheeler, then an engineer, finished an MBA at the London Business School and decided to take a year out for a leisurely backpacking trip around the world, with his wife, before settling back down to earning a living. By the time they reached Australia, however, they'd run out of money and got a taste for the travelling life, to the point where there was no going back. Instead, they wrote a little book about their journey, inspired by all the people who asked them 'How did you do it?' and 'How did you Poms get here?'. They called it *Across Asia on the Cheap*, published it themselves, stapling the pages together on a kitchen table, and found they had enough money from local sales in Sydney to pay for another trip through Asia. This gave them the material for *South-East Asia on a Shoestring*, which has now guided two generations of adventurers through the pleasures and pitfalls of low-budget travel, and they suddenly found they had a business. That was the beginning of Lonely Planet Publications, Wheeler's Australian-based publishing empire, which now has four hundred titles and three hundred employees and sells over three million travel books a year.

The company has always done things differently, not least because bankers and others have never felt happy with a firm that published guides for 'weird people going to weird places'. Wheeler is still away from the business for months every year, travelling, because that is what he likes to do best. When Lonely Planet had been going for twenty-one years, he flew every single member of staff to Australia, at the company's expense, for the big birthday party – including packers from the warehouse in California and secretaries from the London office. It is a big, established success now, but the business still bears the stamp of its founder's enthusiasm and his obviously genuine desire to share it with the travellers who buy his books.

The lessons are clear. If there's something you feel compelled to do with your life, you've got to go for it – or you'll never know if it would have worked. If you make sure the benefit to others is built in, right from the start, you stand a very reasonable chance of being successful and wealthy, not just on the outside but also in the way you feel in yourself.

Chapter 10

Relationships

Be a friend to thyself and others will be so too.
Thomas Fuller, MD

Are you giving what you want to receive?

Julie loves surprises. For her, half the fun of Christmas and birthdays is choosing and giving the most unexpected presents. It's the thought that counts. But it's the surprise element in the thinking that tickles Julie's fancy.

Paul, unfortunately, does not share Julie's love of surprises. He never knows quite how to react and he hates being given things he doesn't want or doesn't like and cannot tactfully dispose of.

Both of them are good, well-meaning people, fond of each other and keen to make each other happy. And each, fatally, is programmed to give what he or she wishes to receive.

Paul drags Julie out to the shops to find just the right present for her, so that she won't be disappointed on her birthday. They end up with the perfect bracelet, but little joy for her and no surprise at all. In his anxiety not to disappoint her, he has ruined the element of surprise that excites her so much.

When Paul's birthday comes round, he thinks Julie must have been so busy at work that she has forgotten it. He has a couple of suggestions for presents he'd really like, but he says nothing. So when Julie gives him her big surprise, it really is a surprise – and it's certainly not what he would have chosen for himself. She has racked her brains to think of something offbeat and unexpected for him, and she is bursting with pleasure at the thought of his delight and astonishment. When the moment comes, he's too kind to say what he thinks, which is 'If she really cared, she'd have asked me what I wanted'. But Julie picks up the lack of enthusiasm and the damage is done, yet again.

The problem, for Julie and Paul, as for many other people in close personal relationships, is that each of them has a mental map of the way the world is – and fails to realise that it is not the only possible map.

Each of them assumes that the other is operating from the same map and the same assumptions. The mismatches happen when they are exchanging presents, when they are planning outings, even when they are making love. If one of a pair of lovers is only excited by surprises and the other always wants to be asked what he or she wants, the scope for frustration is endless. The things Julie needs to signal to her that she is cherished and sexy and attractive are so different from those that carry the same meaning for Paul that there is a real danger of serious misunderstanding. The good news, however, is that once it is pointed out to them that they are both inclined to give what they want to receive, there is likely to be an immediate understanding and improvement.

It's just a matter of realising that people really are radically different, and what works for one person – what proves to them that they are loved or valued – is vitally important to that persons' happiness, though it may make little sense to anyone else.

Home or work, it all comes down to relationships

Enhancing your relationships with NLP is a subject that could easily take up a whole book in its own right. But we have a broader canvas to cover, so we are going to cherry-pick and provide you with just a few key thoughts and techniques that will enable you to make dramatic improvements in the quality of your relationships.

Though we opened the chapter with Julie and Paul and their private, personal responses, the dynamics and processes that govern relationships at work are no different from those in the home.

We know one sales incentive scheme where the monthly prize was a case of wine. Well over half the time it was won by the same individual. He was teetotal and would decline the prize as a matter of principle. He was also getting very disillusioned and eventually quit. As he put it: 'I just didn't feel appreciated.'

Most individuals have one wish list of things they need in their personal relationships and another, parallel, wish list of things they feel they need in their relationships with their employers and their work. Until these have been articulated – or, at least, identified – it is unlikely that the crucial symbols and gestures that mean so much to individual people will be in place.

The point is, of course, that the distinction between personal relationships and work relationships is a false one. All relationships are deeply personal, wherever they occur. We may be able to partly disengage, so that we do not feel work-based slights and conflicts with quite the same raw sensitivity we bring to our intimatc relationships at home, but they still tug at the same levers. No one goes to work to fail, to feel inadequate, to be disliked or to be ignored. So we're always on the lookout for the symbols that might tell us we're appreciated, respected and secure, even while we pretend to operate on the most unemotionally professional plane. It is important for managers, especially, to understand this, because it is the ultimate explanation for many of the most spectacular breakdowns and bust-ups that take place in normally calm and sober workplaces.

'What do I need to do ...?'

When people fail to understand the need to manage relationships, at work and at home, there is always a price to pay. All too often, they end up feeling helpless and hopeless. All the relating they're doing is reactive. Their confidence vanishes and their belief in what is possible in the future shrinks to almost nothing. The problem, then, is that they find themselves wishing and hoping for a change for the better, but are quite unable to do anything about it themselves. The desperate cry of 'When are people going to change so I can be happy?' carries its own inevitable answer. And yet, it is such a little step forward from this passivity to a realistic basis for action.

You don't have to sit around hoping for others to change. NLP provides a simple lever to help you initiate change yourself. The key question is really quite straightforward:

'What do I need to do so that others will naturally want to change, thus increasing their happiness and mine?'

This is the application, if you like, of the win-win theory of management to personal relationships. By applying ingenuity and creativity to the task of aligning your goals and those of the people you need to shift, you are inventing a situation where the forces opposing change just melt away. It is in no one's interest to block it, because everybody's self-interest points in the same direction. By even beginning to focus on the possibility of devising some such solution, you are already starting to move away from passivity towards a less disempowered state. Again, the dynamics of relationships are universal. What works in business works in the home, and vice versa.

The big question for Bob, who feels his marriage is falling apart and wants his wife to love him again, is not, as he tends to think it is, a question about when Vivienne is going to change. Something has caused their problems, and some positive action is going to be needed if the relationship is to be revived. We don't know what Vivienne's point of view is. But we do know that for Bob to get what he wants, something is going to have to change. And if Bob is going to make that change happen, he is going to have to find some point of leverage, within his control, where he can take action to begin to make a difference.

The question Bob needs to be asking himself is a simple one:

'What do I need to do so that she will want to love me again?'

It sounds like a tall order, to think of something that will change Vivienne's mind like this. Yet it is remarkable how often people in this position can provide their own precise and specific answers.

In this particular case, Vivienne wanted to go back to work, for all sorts of reasons, ranging from having more money, wanting a challenge and needing contact with other people, right through to validating her own sense of her place in the world. The big, unspoken agenda item, lurking in the background, was the fact that she also wanted to create the possibility of economic independence for herself, so that she could feel she was making her own free choice about whether to stay with Bob or leave him and make a separate life of her own.

Bob was aware of some of this and had some apprehensive suspicions about the rest. He knew, for example, that Vivienne kept talking about getting a job, though he had, quite logically, pointed out that he earned good money and her present earning power was likely to be low. With his stressful, taxing City job convincing him day in and day out that work was always going to be a battle for survival, shielding Vivienne from such pressures had become a goal he simply took for granted. Yet, to her, this protective care seemed more like a ball and chain – like being put under house arrest for the foreseeable future. Bob was permanently exhausted, bored and boring, with nothing left for life outside work, and the rift between them was widening fast.

If what you are doing isn't working, do something different

When he first faced up to asking himself 'What do I need to do so that Vivienne will want to love me again?', Bob's reaction was a common one. He immediately thought he should be doing more of what he was already doing – working harder, earning more money and trying, even more determinedly, to make Vivienne's life 'easier'. But, of course, more of the same is not a recipe for change. There is a very fundamental NLP guideline that says 'If what you are doing is not working, do something different'. The likelihood of The-Same-Bob-Only-More-So being what Vivienne needed was slim to non-existent.

After focusing strictly on the 'What do I need to do?' question, Bob suddenly recognised, for the first time, that it really was essential for him to change. He suddenly understood that setting himself up so that he could be seen, however unfairly, as Vivienne's jailer was the fast track to disaster. If she wanted to go back to work, he would have to change tack and encourage her to get involved in something she would find stimulating and satisfying. And if he wanted her to love him again, he realised he would have to make himself more interesting, more attractive as a person, and hence more lovable.

This last insight was greeted with a groan. Even Bob had never thought of himself as the world's most fascinating man.

'What am I supposed to do?' he asked. 'Star in a Hollywood epic, grow 6 inches taller or win Wimbledon?'

Clearly, none of this was going to happen. But his sarcastic retort actually pointed the way forward. Hollywood was never going to call, but Bob might consider reviving his former interest in the local amateur dramatic group. He wasn't going to grow taller, but he could certainly choose to do something about shedding the 20lb of flab he had acquired in the previous three years. Winning at Wimbledon might be out of the question, but finding time to play the odd game of tennis with Vivienne wouldn't do either him or their relationship any harm.

There were probably dozens of similar initiatives that Bob could have thought of along these lines. The point is that the apparently daunting feat of finding ways to make himself more interesting and attractive was by no means impossible, once the problem was seen from this point of view. Instead of feeling like a hapless, hopeless, helpless victim, Bob could choose to take positive action to change his situation.

Gradually, he began to think about the relationship differently, until one day he said: 'We can't really have a future together unless I know she's free to go, but chooses to stay. And I'll never know that until she's got her own independent income.' From that moment on, he really supported her in finding a job. She appreciated this new understanding of what was important to her and felt easier in herself with him. She also liked what she saw as Bob 'getting a grip on things again'. That was five years ago and they are still together.

Making X want to do Y: NLP's universal algebra of success

In the commercial arena, the pleasingly symmetrical idea of going for win-win solutions to complex problems has been around for many years, though it could hardly claim to have established itself as the normal way of doing business. The problem is that there don't seem to be all that many situations in which both sides in a negotiation are really particularly interested in win-win, rather than their own immediate gains. Though deals and agreements in which both parties feel pleased and satisfied that they are progressing towards their goals produce dependably stable business relationships, many managers still fail to realise what a significant and profitable long-term advantage this can be.

If both partners are looking for this kind of result right from the start, the task of aligning two sets of objectives is difficult enough. If one of the participants is not inclined to take a co-operative approach, the other has to operate from a situation that has some elements in common with the predicament Bob found himself in. Again, there is no way of forcing the other people involved to change their minds. The change has to happen with their consent or not at all. And again the key question is looking for a point of leverage:

'What do we need to do so that the others will naturally want to change, thus improving their situation and ours?'

At the high corporate level, the answer might be something as radical as suggesting that two companies should swap underperforming subsidiaries, if it appeared that both subsidiaries would gain from the new opportunities available to them in their new homes. There have been some spectacular examples of this in the European plastics and chemical industries, allowing restructuring and rationalisation of overproduction that could never have occurred before the swaps. AT&T and IBM plumped for a similar exchange deal, while MCI WorldCom and Electronic Data Systems swapped assets worth $17 billion, moving 13,000 employees from one payroll to the other.

On a more mundane plane, within a single company, this kind of thinking can lead to solutions to many long-running niggles. The classic case is the accounts department that simply cannot rely on the salesforce to complete the paperwork when an order is taken. In one firm we worked with, this had become a major source of friction. Just nagging the salespeople was not working and not having the information to do the job was causing serious frustration and demotivation in the accounts office. Once more, the same question needed to be asked:

'What do we need to do so that others will naturally want to change, thus improving their situation and ours?'

Or, to put the question in its simplest possible form:

'What do I need to do to make X want to do Y?'

We call this the algebra of success, because once you look at a situation in this way, the answers often seem to pop out almost automatically. In this example, we suggested a very slight modification to the way the company operated its sales bonus system. Instead of bonuses being paid out when a successful sale had been verified by the sales manager, they were now paid, immediately and automatically, when fully completed documentation was received by the accounts office.

The salespeople were happy, because money came through faster and their dockets were never left waiting in the sales manager's in-tray for sign-off. The accounts people got the orderly flow of correct and complete paperwork they needed to make their lives easier. Everybody was a lot happier and the relationships in the office, which had been getting distinctly prickly, moved on to a far more positive footing.

Little things mean a lot

Until the system was changed so that both departments' goals were aligned, the problem in this office was really just blank incomprehension. The sales staff genuinely couldn't believe that order dockets were really important to the people in accounts. The accounts people couldn't understand how salespeople could be so cavalier about the paperwork. To one group, a slip of paper carried meaning and significance. To the other, it was just so much bumf.

As Julie and Paul demonstrated at the beginning of this chapter, the same sort of incomprehension can exist in even the closest personal relationships. Things and actions that have potent and mysterious significance for one partner can mean less than nothing to the other.

Even when people try very hard to tell each other what they want, they often fail to get the message across. Part of the problem here is that people's descriptions of the things they want from their relationships are often couched in abstract terms – in words like love, warmth, appreciation, trust, companionship, security, support, loyalty, honesty, a sense of belonging and the feeling of being needed. You know when these things are there – and when they're not, you can feel their absence cruelly.

Since you can't see, hear or feel the abstract qualities that matter most to people in their relationships, you can only check whether they are actually there in terms of behaviours and symbols.

So behaviours get to be incredibly important. They are the touchstone we use to let us know if our most cherished needs are being met. They tell us if our values — honesty, commitment, feeling cared for and so on — are being honoured or violated.

These behaviours obviously therefore have enormous meaning. They are very individual though, even idiosyncratic. As one woman said: 'I know I'm loved when he puts the palms of his hands on my cheeks and tells me, "I'll never leave".' For her this is the magic formula. And it must be the palms of his hands, not just his fingers.

These little things, then, are really quite enormous.

What does it for you?

Mismatching the gesture, so that you fail to give your partner what he or she sees as the vital external symbol of the deeper qualities in the relationship, happens all the time. But it is often because the partner does not say what he or she needs to feel loved or secure or supported or needed. And if you are the partner, how can you say what it is you need, unless you have discovered this for yourself?

It is actually worth being very direct about this, because it often brings surprising results. Do the following exercise for yourself and then run through it again to find out what special, private symbols hold particular meaning for your partner.

Begin by asking yourself a key question:

'What do I want from this relationship?'

Give yourself time to come up with a generous handful of answers, which may well touch on all sorts of areas – social, emotional, sexual, economic, inspirational or totally unpredictable.

Once you have done this and identified, as clearly as you can, what the most important factors are, you need to find what symbols represent those things for you. Now ask yourself the follow-up question:

'What do I need to see, hear or feel to let me know that my needs have been met?'

For example, if your chief need is to be appreciated, ask yourself: 'What do I need to see, hear or feel to let me know that I am appreciated?' Do not censor your answers, however unexpected or trivial they may seem.

For some people, the behaviours that represent these really important matters can be such minor things that they hardly seem worth mentioning. There are many older mothers for whom being needed is symbolised by the ritual of offering their grown-up children a cup of tea, or a full meal, as soon as they walk in through the front door – and their children's acceptance of the gesture. Some lovers need to be kissed, often, while others get impatient with what to them is such sloppy stuff, and need to be taken out to shows and restaurants to make them feel loved and romantic. In olden times, the average princess needed her knight to slay her a dragon or two to reassure her about the relationship, while today's equivalent might be struggling home on the 5.38 train from town with an unwieldy and oversized bunch of flowers. For some men, it is the loved one's willingness to tolerate hours spent playing or watching sport that confirms that they are loved and accepted for who they are.

Mind-reading is not the answer

People develop their own yardsticks for assessing what is going on around them and for testing whether their impressions are valid and correct. They may not consciously choose their criteria and they may need some coaxing to think about them and articulate what they are. But it is worth everybody's while to do this.

If you know what you want from a relationship and what signals will let you know you've got it, your partner can choose whether or not to act in ways that will send you those signals. That isn't manipulative, on either side. It simply means that instead of playing Blind Man's Buff and risking misinterpreting each other's feelings, you have the opportunity to carry the relationship forward and build into it the elements of reassurance that will make it stronger.

This point is so vitally important for people's personal relationships that it cannot be stressed too much. Love is not the same as mind-reading. Wanting to please another person is not necessarily the same as being able to guess what that person wants at a particular time. Yet many people act as if their partners are being deliberately provocative when they fail to read their minds.

'If he loved me, he'd know – he'd just know' wails the girl in the TV soap opera. 'If I have to tell him what I want, it's not the same.' But the feeling that even a gesture of affection somehow doesn't count if one person has had to tell the other is a recipe for all kinds of misunderstanding.

Once you get into this way of thinking – and many people do – it's hard to get out of it, because it becomes hard to know what's real and what is not. Look where it leads on to. The next step is almost inevitable: 'If I have to tell him, then when he does what I like, how will I know if it's real or if he's just going through the motions?' By this time, the girl is shadow-boxing, creating a situation in which nothing her partner does or doesn't do can possibly be right or be understood at face value.

Now imagine your partner asking you, directly: 'What would you like me to do that would make you feel loved?' How would that be for you? Would it be OK with you to have someone who loved you enough to want to know and to do it? Or does that somehow not count? Because your partner didn't guess that what you wanted was to get away for a walk by the sea or eat breakfast in bed or visit your sister or have your shoulder kissed, does that mean that he or she doesn't really care?

If your test of a good relationship is that the other person should always magically know and be able to meet your every need, you are really asking for telepathy. And that's not realistically on offer in an adult relationship where the other person is a different, separate being, with his or her own history, mysteries and sense of self. Simply becoming aware of the dangers and making a conscious effort to eliminate mind-reading is one of the most immediate and important ways of strengthening and deepening your intimate relationships.

The toolkit for managing your relationships

The key to managing every form of relationship, whether personal or business, is to understand that all relationships end up being what you make them. Whatever the starting points and however unpromising they may look, most relationships can be made to yield positive results, as long as it is understood that they don't just happen. They are always likely to need managing.

Using the techniques outlined in this chapter, you can be clear about what you want from a relationship and what evidence you would need to know you were getting it. Next time a problem arises, first you will understand the importance of being clear about what you want. Second, you will know to ask direct questions about what is wanted on the other side of the relationship, rather than indulging in mind-reading. Third, you will know that your behaviour has meaning to others and you will understand how essential it is to know what are the appropriate behaviours *for this person*, so that you can be sure of sending the right message. This way, you'll be able to use the right signals and symbols to keep the relationship on course. And, finally, you will know how to create change and progress through the algebra of success by asking, 'What do I need to do to make X want to do Y?' These techniques can make a real difference for you – between being on the receiving end of the forces at work in your relationships and being able to manage them to get what you want.

Chapter 11

Work

Every man's work is a portrait of himself.
Samuel Butler

What do you think you're doing?

For many people, work is a tiresome necessity – a question of grinding out a living in an office in town, a waterlogged paddy field or a factory full of noise. But whoever you are, wherever you are, work that does nothing for you but put food on your plate adds up to something close to slavery. There is more to life than that. And there should be more to work than that, too.

Most people realise that they need more than just money from the work they do. Some are fortunate enough to love what they are doing. Others are wary of admitting they really like their work, in case this might somehow put them in a vulnerable position where employers or clients might invite them to have the same enjoyment for rather less money. But that raises interesting questions, too. People mutter enviously about the vast sums of money the top tennis players, footballers, singers and actors are paid, but no one seriously suggests that they should be paid nothing, just because the exercise of their skills is something they enjoy. It is usually only the scale of the rewards that provokes comment.

Unless you live in a police state, you will have some choices about what work you do. Whatever the economy of your area is like, there will be opportunities to work for others or to start new businesses. Yet the sense of powerlessness that comes with feeling trapped by your responsibilities in a job that you do not wish to be doing can make it hard to see the choices open to you. Part of the aim of this chapter is to help you see how you can change your working life for the better – if that is what you need – either by taking radical action or by a gradual but purposeful process of evolution. With the use of selected NLP techniques, you will be able to extend your range of options and get more of what you need out of the time and effort you invest in your work.

Taking stock

The first step is to take stock of yourself and your present work situation. Take a pen and paper and spend a few minutes answering the following questions. Your answers do not need to be essays. They can be written in note form, if you like, as long as they are detailed and specific enough to mean something useful when you come back to them later.

Jot down one or two answers to each of the questions:

1. What is important to you about what you do now?
2. What would you rather be doing?
3. What is important about what you would rather be doing?
4. What were your dreams and ambitions earlier in life and as a child?
5. How could you bring these into play now?

You will have noticed that the last two questions ask for a different type of answer from the others. All the rest are to do with now and with your needs for the future. Question 4, at least on the surface, seems to be about the past. But of course it's not. Somewhere inside you, there is still that little child or that idealistic young adult who wanted to do something special or change the world.

Gill was working in an advertising agency. Originally she'd been attracted to the advertising world by its 'glamour' as she saw it. When we met her she was taking stock. Her answers to these questions made it very clear how a new direction could produce a lot more of what she wanted.

What was important to her about what she was presently doing was, as she said: 'Being well paid and well liked. Every day is different and I get to make significant decisions.' What would she rather be doing? 'I'd rather be working with people who had some real creative flair and were making something fresh.' Clearly there was some mismatch here. Her answer to Q3, 'What is important about what you would rather be doing?' explained why. 'The arts and that world have always fascinated me,' she said, 'and I'd feel more alive if I was involved in making them happen.' In answer to Q4 she talked of how when she was young she had desperately wanted to be a ballet dancer. In reply to Q5 she said: 'I'm too old to be a ballet dancer! But I realise I'd love to have some contact with the dance world especially.'

Gill left the advertising agency and now she's involved in promoting corporate sponsorships of arts events. In her spare time she's helping set up a local children's ballet school where she lives. 'Who knows, we might even be able to make a business out of it!' she said.

Somewhere, there is a part of you that may never have entirely let go of that old ambition. If what you do for a living can somehow be reunited with the themes of those early ambitions, the results can be deeply satisfying. It is like coming home to a half-forgotten part of you. Many people have had the experience of seeing childhood ambitions damped down and gradually whittled away by reality and circumstance. But it is a mistake to turn your back completely on the memory of them.

Who's that person in your CV?

If you look back over the answers you've written down in the last few minutes, you will get a picture of the person you are – or, at least, one important set of facets of that person. It won't be complete, but it should be recognisably you.

Now look through your drawer or your files and find a copy of your CV or résumé. This may be years out of date, because you have had no cause to modernise it while working in the same job for a long time. It may be a current version, cooked up fairly recently in a bid to change your job, and quite possibly heavily skewed in the direction that was likely to catch a possible new employer's eye. But whether the CV you dig out is old or new, written for the world at large or targeted at a particular position with a specific employer, you can be sure of one thing. It won't say much at all about who you are or what you're like.

Assuming you have not included outright lies, your CV will contain a true, factual account of your qualifications, experience and work history. Yet it will still tell the reader almost nothing that he or she really needs to know about you.

A CV is such a partial and incomplete description of a person that anyone who sets much store by it is either naïve or very cynical indeed about people. And corporations do strange things with them anyway – we once heard it suggested in a hard-pressed human resources department that all applications from people with names beyond F in the alphabet should be binned straight away, in order to leave a pool of roughly 20 per cent of the applicants and move economically forward to the next stage of the selection process.

You can't do much to counter that sort of thinking if your name is Gates or Harvey-Jones. But consciously working on your CV is something that makes a lot of sense to many young, career-minded and ambitious people. They change employers and volunteer for individual projects with one eye on how all this is going to look when it's written down in the formal CV or on the job application form.

In the case of the really ambitious young manager, being able to tick off all the right boxes (a bit of overseas experience here, the launch of a product in a new market there, or driving through a downsizing programme, for example) is seen as the springboard for the leap into the boardrooms of the upper echelons of international business. But, whatever experience holes you need to plug, we would suggest you aim to gradually bring your CV into line with who you are, rather than bending who you are to fit the demands of human resources departments and CV-sorting computers.

Time to write your Secret CV

For all their inadequacies, CVs do have their uses. With your own CV in front of you now, you can fill in the important gaps.

To do this, take up your pen and paper again and write, for the first time in your life, your Secret CV. This is a potentially open-ended task and you might want to come back to it later, but allow, say, fifteen minutes for a first stab at it. Your Secret CV, the one you will never show to anyone else, relates your work history to the real you.

The entries in your public CV will be useful as memory-joggers, but what you are looking for in this exercise is six answers that are not a matter of public record.

The aim of the Secret CV is to highlight aspects of yourself and your potential. You may be surprised how readily six untapped talents or unacknowledged strengths come to mind. Write them down, but don't feel you have to stop or make a choice if you think of more than six answers. Do it now.

Six things I know about myself, in relation to work, that do not show up yet on my official CV:

1. ....

2. ....

3. ....

4. ....

5. ....

6. ....

The 'yet' is there because these are exactly the sort of qualities that you know you possess but that have hitherto gone unrecognised. If your present job starts to deliver more of what you need or you change jobs to something more involving and fulfilling, these will probably be brought to the surface and become visible in your work. At the moment, though, your answers will define almost exactly the differences between what your boss thinks he or she knows about you and what your close friends know you are capable of.

Jim had been self-employed for some years, but just wasn't making the kind of money he needed now to support either his ex-wife and children or his new life. He was starting to feel anxious and his sleep was not like it used to be. Reluctantly he started thinking about becoming an employee – it wasn't much good having your own business if you didn't make any money.

And then a strange thing happened. Within the space of seven days he was approached twice with job offers. Both came about through clients who'd mentioned his name to others. Both offered to give him some financial stability, but now he felt stuck because he didn't know how to choose. The money for each job was about the same, so that wasn't going to give him an easy answer.

One post was with a soft drinks company and their publicity department. It would involve travel, which he loved, and promised further promotion. The other was playing a key role in the launch of a new business magazine. Both posts were initially one-year contracts.

After Jim had completed his Secret CV he was able to make the choice very easily. He thought they were both really good jobs but now he was in no doubt. Here's his list:

1. Good-humoured and good with people
2. Lots of stamina
3. Careful about details
4. Full of ideas about how to grow a business
5. Able to teach skills to others
6. Interested in computing and the Internet

In his words: 'I hadn't realised how important these six things were. Suddenly the magazine seems the way to go – I'll be taking on a job that fits with me much better. I feel like I'm going in the right direction again.'

Writing the Secret CV is quite different from working on your formal CV. This time round you need to be unblushingly honest, with no false modesty about your talents and capabilities. You are looking for positive traits and potential, so nothing you write here is going to make it an incriminating document.

If you are a sociable, outgoing, friendly sort of person and you spend your working days silently peering down a microscope in a pathology lab somewhere, it doesn't necessarily mean you are in the wrong job. If your scientific skills are a source of pride and pleasure to you, you may well be happy to let your sociable side hibernate while you are at work and make up for this when you are away from the bench with your friends and family. While everything else, at home and at work, is going smoothly, this is a perfectly sensible way to live. But if tensions start to build up, you may find that seven hours a day of effective isolation is not good for you. The mere fact that your talent for warmth and communication does not have a channel to express itself in your work might then be frustrating.

You only have to watch an injured sports star chafing on the sidelines for weeks while a broken leg or muscle injury slowly heals to see how agonising the inability to use your potential can be. Professional athletes can be earning huge salaries for 'doing nothing' while their injuries mend, but it is patently obvious that in almost every case they are itching to get back into action as soon as possible.

The quiet, thoughtful person who falls into a job as a hairdresser, a telesales operator, an estate agent or a teacher may well find that other people's expectations of a constant flow of words make life uncomfortable. The chatterbox who takes the job in the library may face an equally awkward mismatch between his or her personality and the working environment. So it is always worth thinking seriously about how much of the real you fits in naturally with the demands of a new job before you commit yourself. Will you have to suppress some parts of your personality and exaggerate others to make a go of it? And, if so, is it worth it for you? Your Secret CV will help to bring some of these issues out into the daylight, so that you can take realistic career decisions with your eyes wide open.

In this way you get to be congruent. And the more congruent you are the more you will get out of your work.

The case of the serial publican

Carrying out this kind of personal audit on yourself is not always a recipe for a quiet life. It can sometimes lead people to make bold and imaginative career switches, as they suddenly realise their time is slipping away and they are spending it doing things that are just not right for them. We know one telephone engineer who gave it all up to become a photographer, while another took advantage of a redundancy package to set up in business as a restorer of vintage cars. And we watched in awe, some years ago, as Janet, a senior accountant, chucked in her job and reinvented herself in a new career that perfectly suited both her moneywise skills and her friendly, extrovert nature – as a pub entrepreneur.

She would home in on a run-down, or even closed-down, public house and hit it like a whirlwind, redecorating, refurbishing and re-targeting it to suit whatever market opportunity she spotted in the immediate area. Over eighteen months or two years, she'd get it re-established as a thriving, demonstrably profitable business and then sell out to one of the many people who dream of taking over a popular, well-run pub. Each time, Janet and her sister, who worked in partnership with her, would reckon to double their capital.

They worked extraordinary hours and put tremendous energy into each of the pubs. But they loved doing it. They loved the sociable, convivial nature of the business – the people, the celebrations, even the late nights – and the way they could measure their progress, almost week by week, as their turnover built up. And, though it was always a wrench to walk away, they loved the year or so's break they would take after selling one pub and before getting down to the task of identifying the next candidate for their turnaround activities. Janet had never been particularly engaged in her work as an accountant. As a serial publican, she found a niche that involved every part of her and suited her down to the ground.

If there are parts of you that you are having to deny or that are not being used in your job or business, use the things that have surfaced in your Secret CV to work towards defining your dream job.

Don't be restricted by the usual assumptions that you must do what you trained to do. Janet's disciplined financial skills were an asset few publicans could match – and they stood her in good stead when it came to producing the evidence of a healthy, attractive business that buyers were looking for. Yet she would never have dreamed, when she was revising for her accountancy finals, that she was acquiring the qualifications that would fit her to spend her life in a succession of pubs. If you have developed specialist skills or knowledge, life often throws up some indirect or completely unexpected way you can make your expertise work for you.

Dream your dream job – then find it

If you are beautiful, cheerful, dextrous or funny by nature, or unusually tall or strong or supple or blessed with fast reactions, or clever or musical or good at languages or able to draw, you start with advantages that may have some role to play in your career choices. But whatever gifts and abilities you have, you may well have to combine them with learned skills and expertise to create a package that can be slotted into a particular niche in the labour market. If you can do this, the sky is the limit.

In the 1940s, Esther Williams combined her Olympic-standard swimming ability, a pleasant face and some acting talent to make a fortune as Hollywood's Million Dollar Mermaid. In the 1990s, a young French scientist called Sophie Labbé discovered that she could combine her chemistry degree with an unusually sharp sense of smell to become one of the world's top perfumers, creating fragrances like Givenchy's Organza and Armani's bestselling Emporio Uomo. 'I didn't know there was any such job,' she told one interviewer, 'until I read about it in *Elle*.'

There is an extraordinary range of weird and wonderful jobs around, many of which call for unusual combinations of attributes. And the total number of careers that you can choose from is growing all the time. Very few old trades disappear completely. Blacksmiths have been doing well recently and we know one young thatcher who makes an excellent living from his craft, criss-crossing the country to repair and replace porches and roofs, and keeping in touch with his customers by mobile phone.

Yet, at the same time, there are completely new careers – for Web site designers, gas and electricity brokers in the UK, and snowboarding instructors, to name just a few – that have existed for only a few years. Every bit of new legislation or new technology has the potential to create a new niche. Every twist of public taste creates the chance to fill a new gap. Where did London's Thai restaurants spring from? Was it just the football World Cup of 1998 that triggered the opening of sports bars, with wide-screen television projectors, across half of Europe? Every time there is change, there is the possibility that a new opportunity will open up for someone with your unique profile and mix of talents. And the more clearly unique you can make that profile, the more chance you have of making the opportunity work for you.

With the help of your Secret CV, you can make sure you do not fail to recognise your dream job, if the opportunity to take it or create it ever occurs. If you stop and think about it now, letting your imagination play with the strengths and attributes you have acknowledged in your Secret CV, you will be more alert to the possibilities that may be open to you.

Imagine the dream job that would use as many of your strengths as possible.

This is the job that uses the whole you – and that, ideally, could not be done well by anyone without your unique combination of skills and personality. If that were the case, you would be in a seller's market and could name your own price and set out your own terms and conditions. If your dream job exists, it is worth going for it for the long-term pay-offs of fulfilment and satisfaction, just as much as for the money. If it doesn't exist, bear in mind the possibility that social or technological changes might bring it into being or that you might be able to create the opening to build a career or a business around whatever you are most suited to doing. But first you've got to have a dream.

You've got to be ready to change direction

The clearer you are about what you've got to offer, the more likely you are to spot the chance to capitalise on it, even if it means switching direction in mid-stream. Flexibility and the wit to spot the opportunity when it opens up for you are almost as important as talent. UK comedians Billy Connolly, Jasper Carrott and Richard Digance were all established folk musicians before they realised the instruments were getting in the way of the laughs. Madonna was a dancer, until she decided singing might be a better way to achieve her ambitions. Our friend Sally ran a computer training company, until she got involved in importing weatherproofed timber for sundecks from New Zealand and Scandinavia. For several years, she ran the two businesses side by side, gradually tapering off one in favour of the other, until it became clear that the decking company was where her fortune was going to be made.

What you do is your own business – and all businesses, big and small, benefit from watching the world around them and being ready to reinvent themselves if necessary. Even giants have to change. A Woolworths store today is very different from one of twenty years ago and it is more or less par for the course for a small business to start by addressing one market and then develop so that it either specialises in one segment of that market or gradually shifts across to serve a different set of customers. This is why it is so important to be clear about what your own goals are, in order to avoid confusing ends and means.

If what you are doing now is only a means to an end, there is likely to be a time when the best route towards that end is no longer doing more of what you're already doing. Just working harder for longer may not do it. If at first you don't succeed, the old advice to grit your teeth and 'try, try again' is sometimes misguided, if it spurs you on to keep banging your head against a wall. Trying suggests earnest effort, which is no substitute for real achievement. If you are trying to do something, you have yet to master the art of doing it. That's fine, if you are learning as you go, but sometimes people get stuck in trying. On the whole, you would do better to rewrite the motto to read: 'If at first you don't succeed, do something different'. NLP is very suspicious of the word 'try'. If someone says 'I'll try to call you tomorrow', you would be unwise to stay in all day, waiting for the phone to ring. There are no points for repeated, persistent trying and failing. So stop doing it and do something different. Instead, follow the most basic process for moving from failure to success. There are just four steps to it:

1. Stop doing what has failed and do something different.
2. Notice what happens when you do that.
3. Modify your behaviour in the light of the feedback you get.
4. Do something different and better again.

Think of this process as a feedback loop that is continually taking you closer and closer to your goal. To manage your career and your life successfully, you don't necessarily need to get things right first time. What you do need is robust, usable processes, like this one, that will reliably move you forward in the direction you want to go.

It's what you do that counts

The quotation at the head of this chapter neatly sums up one of the great truths about work. Samuel Butler was right: every man's work is a portrait of himself, as is every woman's, paid or unpaid. But it can be an unflattering, warts-and-all portrait, if it shows a person crammed into a strait-jacket and giving up on the struggle for engagement, meaning and personal satisfaction. The person who settles for second best, for work that is not a reflection of what he or she is, as well as what he or she can do, may well be opting out in ways that can be dangerously dispiriting.

Work – in the sense of paid employment – can often be one of the things that give life purpose and meaning. It doesn't have to be, though. There are many people who do energetic, constructive work for charities and other worthwhile causes, in their own time, funded by uninspiring day jobs that use little of their potential. So you might say it's what you do that counts, not necessarily what you do for a living.

But, if you're going to be in control of your life, just consider how much of it is taken up with working. When you decide to manage your life, it's essential to set your day-to-day priorities to reflect the realities of what is important to you. If you get this right, so that what you spend your time doing feels good and valid to you, your work or your business or your job can be one of the most positive elements in your life. William Faulkner summed up the inevitable importance of work in people's lives in a memorable observation. 'The only thing a man can do for eight hours a day, day after day, is work,' he said. 'You can't eat eight hours a day nor drink for eight hours a day nor make love for eight hours.' And since he's right, we can't afford to get it wrong.

Chapter 12

Joie de Vivre

Some folk want their luck buttered.
Thomas Hardy

Joie de vivre? It's a learnable skill

Joie de vivre is not about ecstacy or ownership or the sensational thrills of the big, set-piece moments in your life. It is about feeling alive, feeling good, feeling engaged, every day of your life. It is about being alive to the little pleasures and minor joys of everyday existence and being able to draw fuel and sustenance from them, in very ordinary, unspectacular ways, to carry you through any problems you meet.

Some people have the knack of doing this spontaneously. Like a solar-powered watch or calculator, they only need to see a glimpse of sunlight to set them up for the day. For most of us, though, it is an art that we need to practise and develop. The good news, however, is that there is nothing particularly difficult about learning. You can do it in a number of straightforward and systematic ways – and this chapter will show you how.

How will you be happy if you hit the jackpot?

People often assume that something big has to change in their lives before they can feel alive and feel good a lot of the time. You hear them say it: 'Now if I were to win the lottery, ah, then everything would be different.'

The good news is that you don't actually have to wait for a miracle. You don't have to wait to get lucky. You can start making your own luck. We're going to stay with the lottery fantasy for a while and see how this all works.

Nobody in the world wants luck for its own sake. It's no good being lucky if it doesn't make you happy. As the old song says, 'All the money in the world is spent on feeling good.'

Winning the lottery can't buy you happiness, but it can buy you a Ferrari, or a sea-going catamaran, or a big house on a hillside somewhere. Then the question is whether the thing it has bought you has the capacity to make you happy. We all know the clichés that tell you money doesn't bring happiness, but there's little evidence to indicate that the absence of it is any kind of recipe for lasting bliss. So let's look at what you could do to make yourself really happy if you did suddenly have millions at your disposal – and then work back towards strategies for getting the same sort of pleasures in less costly ways, until you do.

Our advice to lottery winners would be just the same as our advice to everyone else. Even if you have millions sloshing around in the bank, you've got to work a bit at noticing what really makes you feel good. With any luck, there will be many answers to this, depending partly on the sort of moods you are in. But the answers may not be what you expect. We know of one millionaire who has found his chief pleasure in having money is the fact that he can now afford to spend more time in a bare room, meditating. What the money has done is make it possible to go to a variety of interesting, wild and remote places to find suitable bare rooms to meditate in. Knowing he will not want to meditate for more than two or three hours at a time, he chooses locations where he will want to get out and be physically active, walking, climbing or swimming, during the rest of each day.

At the other extreme, there are people who take up skiing or flying and find these activities so engrossing and exhilarating that they never want to come down. Some choose to pit themselves against mountains, while others are drawn to motor or powerboat racing. Anita Roddick, of Body Shop, found that her success and fortune gave her scope to go anywhere she wanted and indulge her passion for travelling and exploration in the Third World. Several British millionaires have set up and financed their own cricket teams, out of love for a complex sport where simply playing seems to matter far more than winning or losing.

Please yourself

What all these people have in common is some sort of understanding of what turns them on as individuals. They are all looking for different kinds of satisfaction or stimulation and what suits one would be emphatically wrong for another.

They may be seeking calm and serenity, excitement with a spice of danger, the physical sensations of speed and power or the stimulus of a competitive challenge. Some will be using their activities to forge social links with other people interested in the same things. Some will get all the pleasure they need from stretching their own physical or mental capacities.

What is guaranteed, right from the start, is that the only way to find your own happiness is to know what is pleasing to you. If you do ever win the lottery, by all means listen to other people's recommendations and try everything that appeals to you. But it is essential that you continue to assess all your new experiences by your own standards of what works for you. (And by the way, while you're waiting for your numbers to come up, you might want to start doing this anyway.) If you try to fit in with other people's ideas of what's exciting or glamorous, or fun, you might end up one day on a golf course or a yacht or a cruise liner somewhere, feeling jaded and let down and asking yourself: 'Just who am I really doing this for?'

Lessons from the lottery

Whether you have won your millions yet or not, there are two important lessons to be learnt from looking at the experiences of real people who have won – or, more frequently, inherited – large sums of money.

Lesson 1: It's what you do – not what you own – that makes the difference.

It definitely seems to be what you do that matters, far more than what you possess, and the sudden arrival of ample amounts of money should increase the range of choices open to you. Although many lottery winners immediately go out and buy themselves one real treat that they have always wanted, most find that the best approach to all the new choices is to postpone making major purchases for a while. Most of life's luxuries can be rented, hired or chartered and assuming ownership often brings unwanted complications in its wake. Deep-sea fishing in the Caribbean may be a tempting prospect, but if you buy the boat, what's going to happen to it for the ten months of the year when you are thousands of miles away?

Simply possessing doesn't seem to deliver. But figuring out what you want to *do* with your time and the rest of your life has a huge impact.

Lesson 2: Look after the hours and the weeks will look after themselves.

The second lesson is that every minute counts. Your personal happiness is likely to be determined by how you feel, minute by minute and hour by hour, as well as week by week. There seems to be absolutely no correlation between the amount of wealth available to you and how you feel from moment to moment. So why wait? Consider what's going to enable you to feel good and more alive right now.

Learn to value the moment

Truly happy people – the ones with the naturally sunny and positive way of appreciating daily life that we call *joie de vivre* – make the most of those good moments. They notice them, savour them and refuse to take them for granted.

If you ask happy people, at the end of a busy day, 'What were the things that gave you pleasure today?' they will usually be able to reel off a surprisingly long list of small delights. These may include very simple and specific sensory pleasures. They will list things like 'the smell of new bread as I went past the bakery', 'the colour of the clouds when the rain stopped' or 'that toddler's smile as she squelched in the mud with her boots', alongside the more 'sophisticated' pleasures of a restaurant meal or a good bottle of wine.

Recognising this kind of spontaneous, everyday pleasure is very important in setting the overall tone of a person's day. If you can find small-scale delights in everyday living and everyday people, you are always going to be less tempted to wish your life away waiting for the weekend or pining for your holiday or the next big occasion. The whole texture of your days becomes happier and more positive. Just as a grumpy ticket collector or traffic warden (or spouse, for that matter) can get you off to a bad start, it may only take a tiny flash of good humour or an unexpected card in the post or a ray of sunlight through your bedroom window to make you feel good about the day.

The people who seem to have a natural talent for enjoying such moments thrive on everyday encounters. Like the great whales, they can get the nourishment they need from the krill and plankton of life's ocean. But it is important to know that this ability to get full value out of simple pleasures is something you can train yourself to develop. If you go through your day alive to the possibility of identifying and appreciating all the small and fleeting events and moments that make you feel good, you will find you attract more of them. And this is something you can start learning now.

Your ten-day Diary of Delights

If you choose to, you can change your life over the next ten days. This may sound like an outrageous claim, but it is one you can test for yourself, surprisingly easily. Some ideas have enormous impact. There are some ideas that can change the way you think and, through that, the way you feel, and even, through that, the way you relate to other people. This is one of them:

If you want to enjoy more of the big things in life – success, fun, love, satisfaction and whatever else you crave – you should start with the little things.

There is no better place to start than right here. All you have to do, for the next few days, is to track the opportunities for feeling good that you encounter in your daily life. We recommend a ten-day experiment, by the end of which you are likely to have accumulated enough detailed evidence to leave you in no doubt.

Do it properly, though. You may be sceptical about what is happening if you do not have a day-by-day record, in writing, to refer back to. This is what you should do:

1.   Buy yourself a small notebook or make use of a spare diary and carry it with you all the time for the next ten days.
2.   Each time you notice a small pleasure or instant of delight during the day, jot down a note to remind you of it.
3.   Each evening, look through your notes and pick out the ten delights you remember most vividly from the day.

At first, you may find it hard to recall ten of these special moments, because you are not used to registering them. Indeed, it is probably a good idea to start now and set a benchmark for yourself by casting your mind back over the past twenty-four hours and trying to pick out ten pleasures you experienced during that period. Because you have not been consciously watching out for them and the question has been sprung on you, ten may seem a rather demanding target. Yet there will have been far more than ten candidates during the twenty-four-hour period, as you will readily agree if you come back and read this section again after completing your ten-day diary. If you compare the ease with which you fill your ten slots on the last day of this exercise with the struggle you may have now, you will probably be astonished at the change a few days can bring.

The difference, of course, is all to do with the incredible unconscious sophistication of the human brain. Brains are very clever. Once they are tuned in and looking for something specific in their experience of each day, they will hunt for it ingeniously and relentlessly. Remember what it's like when you decide on a particular model of car – suddenly the roads seem to be swarming with that particular model. That is because your brain is now sorting for a very particular thing which you have made stand out from all the others, because of your interest and enthusiasm. We suck in so much information and sensation every day that one of the brain's most impressive functions is the way it gets rid of things. Without any obvious direction from us, it stores a selective record of experience, tagging the things that it thinks we are likely to want to refer back to and letting a lot of other images and inputs fade quickly into the background. Once your brain knows you are on the lookout for a new class of information – everyday delights – it will sort for suitable candidates all the time.

By the end of the ten-day period, you will find that ten delights a day is no great target at all. This will not necessarily be because your life has actually taken a huge turn for the better. It is simply that the disciplined framework of the Diary of Delights helps you re-calibrate your response to experience, so that you operate on a more fine-grained level, picking up on what would previously have been dismissed as unimportant. But that is exactly the point. A key part of the art of being happy and having *joie de vivre* is living the pleasure of the moment. But you can only do this if you notice it.

What is your pleasure?

It may be a corny old piece of folk wisdom, but the saying that one man's meat is another man's poison applies just as much to the kinds of little pleasures we appreciate as it does to our major choices, such as careers, partners, hobbies and lifestyles. Yet many people have never paused to think about what they particularly like and enjoy, even at the most basic sensory level. We are

equipped with the physical capacity to enjoy with each of our
senses – to get pleasure from seeing, hearing, feeling, tasting and
smelling. But a look at the hundred pleasures accumulated in
your own Diary of Delights over the ten-day period will probably reveal straight away that your particular pleasures tend to
cluster around one or two of these sense channels.

To illustrate the point, let's take a look at some extracts from
a single day's notes compiled by someone whose Diary of
Delights covered a weekend break in Paris:

— having a lie-in in the huge, comfortable bed in our hotel
— smelling the rich aroma of coffee beans as breakfast was
   prepared (by someone else!!)
— seeing the newly-cleaned towers of Notre Dame
— eating a sensational strawberry ice-cream from
   Bertillon's, on the Ile de la Cité
— gazing into the eyes of the Mona Lisa in the Louvre (what
   does that look mean?)
— hearing the world's worst accordion player busking near
   the Pompidou Centre
— looking out across the rooftops from Montmartre in the
   evening.

What is interesting about these delights is that they are spread
more or less equally across the senses – seeing, hearing, tasting,
feeling and smelling. Only one sense – sight – is slightly over-
represented. Here is a person able to experience pleasure
through all the senses. But this is quite unusual. Most people
have a marked tendency to favour one or two of their senses as
their principal sources of pleasure and delight. And this often
narrows the possibilities for feeling good.

In contrast to these metropolitan pleasures, you might have
chosen to spend some time walking in the hills. You, too, might
have registered a fairly even spread of pleasures across the five

senses. But your list could be very different. You might have enjoyed the sight of a tumbling waterfall, the sounds of birds calling above you, the feel of the sun on your back, the taste of fresh bread when you reached your destination and the smell of a wood fire as you ate your evening meal. Wherever you are, there is always likely to be a full range of stimuli with the potential to delight all the senses. But what you derive from this mass of signals from the outside world will largely depend on what you are sorting for.

Potentially pleasurable sensory information is coming at us all, all the time. It certainly doesn't only happen when we go away or take a break from our normal domestic life. Indeed, time spent alone with your partner, sleeping or awake, may well provide an ample range of sensory pleasures, spanning most, if not all, of the five sense channels.

As a rule, people do not know, let alone choose, which of the sensory channels they are most attuned to. The designer, the musician, the juggler, the cook and the perfume-blender may deliberately work to develop and refine particular senses, but for most other people it is not a matter of conscious choice. If you can discover more about yourself in this respect, by referring back to your Diary of Delights, and begin to recognise where you seem to find the most pleasure in small or incidental things, you can get more of what you want and spend more of your time feeling happy.

If you then start to cultivate your other senses, you'll open up a whole new world of pleasure for yourself.

The secret of being happy

If you want to *be* happy, there is a trick to it. The trick is simply to maximise the number of times each day you *feel* happy. So how do you do this? For the moment, let's rule out all the easy and obvious ways like major occasions, social events, treats and outings. You already know about these. Instead, concentrate on the simple pleasures you enjoy in your life. These modest, unspectacular delights are particularly important because they are much more frequent. They also tend to be cheap, self-generated and available without too much pre-planning or co-operation from other people.

They come in many forms. As one husband remarked: 'It never fails to amaze me just how much pleasure my wife gets from needlepoint.' Hobbies are people's own chosen ways of spending their time and increasing the stream of opportunities for small, personal delights. If other people's hobbies sometimes seem unexciting, pointless or unproductive to you, that's irrelevant. They know what they like doing and they're doing it.

You can see just how much pleasure these activities can deliver when you consider how people will choose experiences that might otherwise be considered quite unpleasant. You need to be choosing to play rugby to get any pleasure at all from being buried in the mud under a pile of boots and bodies. Winter gardeners will garden until their fingers turn numb and summer joggers will jog until passers-by wonder whether to call an ambulance.

In the light of your Diary of Delights, with the new evidence it gives you about which sense channels you respond most vividly to and derive most pleasure from, you can often make better choices about what you do with your time. It may be just a question of how you spend a spare ten minutes at lunchtime. But if this is the only part of a particular day that feels like your own time, it is important for you to get something positive out of it. Think about the brief pleasures recorded in your diary and see whether there is something similar that you could enjoy in this short window of opportunity. We knew a woman who worked in a legal office on the third floor of a tall modern office block in

Central London. Every lunchtime, without fail, she carried out the same ritual. Whatever else she was doing, she always set aside a couple of minutes to take the high-speed lift to the very top of the building and look out over the whole of the city. Then she'd come down, refreshed and with her batteries recharged, and plough straight back into her work for the rest of the day. It didn't work for her colleagues, when they tried it, but it did work for her.

You may have your own little rituals and pleasures that give you private moments of joy or boost your spirits when your energy is flagging. If you are not conscious of having any, look through your Diary of Delights again, and see if you can spot the patterns and themes that link your most enjoyable moments. You may realise, for example, that a lot of your pleasures have a social element and require the presence of other people. Or that they are often related to travelling somewhere. Or that you tend to savour stillness and moments of quiet privacy. You may be perfectly well aware of these preferences already. But you may be surprised by some of the patterns and connections that catch your eye. If so, make a note of them and consider how you could spend more of your time in the sort of situation where your magic moments are likely to occur.

In the same way, the new data about yourself gleaned from the Diary of Delights may be particularly useful when it comes to some of your bigger decisions. It can provide extra information to help you in assessing job offers or business opportunities, choosing where to live or deciding what sort of destination to pick for your main holiday of the year. If your Diary of Delights has drawn your attention to the pleasure you take in tactile things, that may well be a reason for holidaying in a warm place, where your body will not be wrapped up in heavy clothing all the time. If your Diary of Delights featured many moments of visual pleasure, a trip to somewhere with spectacular landscapes or old and picturesque buildings will probably be a more inspired choice than a holiday on a flat beach or in a modern city.

Don't fight it, feel it

There is no doubt that the revelations from the ten-day Diary of Delights have helped many people focus on the detail of what they enjoy and start to plan their activities to ensure that they can feel good as often as possible. But you can only plan so much. The biggest benefit, for most people, is the way you get into the habit of sorting for and savouring the little, everyday, unexpected, opportunistic pleasures that come your way – wherever you are and whatever you are doing.

Before the end of the diary period, many people report that they are noticing so many little delights around them that their experience of life has taken a radical turn for the better. Instead of worrying about how to be happier, they find that they are spending more of their time *just being happy*. This steady infusion of moments of happiness, drip, drip, dripping into your life, is an irresistible force. But don't worry. You can handle it.

Coda

There won't be much point in managing your life more effectively if you don't feel good. And to feel good you really need to manage how you are in yourself.

This is an ongoing process. The NLP tools in this book can make all the difference. And there are lots more. But quantity won't really do it.

Everything we've introduced you to you can start doing now. And that's the difference that will make the difference.

Starting to put these principles into practice is like setting out on a journey. But it's a journey you don't have to make on your own. If you would like to explore with others or get some direct hands-on experience you might consider taking an NLP training course. You will find details in Resources – Where to Next?, p. 196.

Either way, the more you begin to manage yourself, the more you will have a life of your own choosing.

We very much hope that you will use, and enjoy using, these NLP tools to manage yourself, and manage your life.

And finally – do let us know how you get on. You can reach us through:

www.nlp-community.com
or *http://members.aol.com/shircore*

Resources – Where To Next?

If you have found this book of interest you will benefit tremendously from actually experiencing our NLP trainings.

Because NLP is skill-based, you can learn a lot in a hands-on training programme that gives you the opportunity to practise the how-tos.

International Teaching Seminars is the UK market leader in quality NLP training. It focuses on the practical applications of NLP and offers a number of different programmes and formats, including:

NLP Practitioner Training – a comprehensive programme leading to internationally recognised practitioner certification. No previous training required.

First Principles – a three-day introduction based on the best-selling book *Principles of NLP* by Ian McDermott and Joseph O'Connor.

Professional Development Programme – divided into two short three-day programmes:
Leadership: how to clarify where to go next in your life
Advanced Presentation Skills: how to use NLP to revolutionise the way you come across

---

Free Information on NLP Training

If you would like to receive a free brochure about NLP training please call International Teaching Seminars on:
(from inside UK): 0207 247 0252   Fax: 0207 247 0242
(from outside UK): +44 207 247 0252   Fax: +44 207 247 0242

Or write to:
International Teaching Seminars
19 Widegate Street
London E1 7HP
England

The Internet

Read articles about NLP applications, enjoy book extracts, download NLP software, get full details on upcoming trainings and NLP books and audiotapes at:

www.nlp-community.com

Index

About the authors

Ian McDermott is a leading trainer, consultant and author in the field of NLP, systems thinking and personal development. His books have been translated into 15 languages. In 1994 he was made an International NLP Diplomate in recognition of his contribution to the field.

As Director of Training for International Teaching Seminars, he has made the practical benefits of NLP available to thousands of people through public and in-house programmes. As a consultant, he works with many FTSE-100 and Fortune 500 corporations including Cable & Wireless, NatWest, Prudential, TSB, Shell, British Telecom and Coca-Cola.

Ian is also a UKCP registered psychotherapist. Both personally and through ITS Executive Coaching he and his colleagues use NLP to deliver rapid change easily to a wide range of people.

A regular contributor to radio, television and the national press, Ian enjoys speaking to a wide range of organisations including Ashridge Management College, the Institute of Personnel and Development and The Industrial Society right through to the Traditional Acupuncture Society and Marriage Care.

Ian McDermott has written many other books, including:

Principles of NLP (Thorsons, 1996)
NLP and Health (Thorsons, 1996)
Practical NLP for Managers (Gower, 1997)
The Art of Systems Thinking (Thorsons, 1997)
(all with Joseph O'Connor)
Develop Your Leadership Qualities (Time-Life, 1995)
Take Control of Your Life (Time-Life, 1996)
(with Joseph O'Connor and others)
NLP and the New Manager (Orion, 1998)
(with Ian Shircore)

Ian McDermott can be contacted through *www.nlp-community.com*

Ian Shircore is an author, management coach and marketing communications consultant. He has worked with the Treasury, London Business School and the International Herald Tribune and has had a fruitful fifteen-year association with BT and the telecoms industry.

He believes technologies like the Internet and new knowledge about how we work are combining to create the preconditions for explosive change. He foresees a new Industrial Revolution and a total reshaping of the way we live and work together.

Ian Shircore has written several other books, including:

Treasure Hunting (Macdonald, 1980)
Right for Your Reader: a painless style guide for Managers (BT, 1994)
Smart Office: 11 steps to the user-friendly office (Bloomsbury, 1996)
(with Judith Verity)
NLP and the New Manager (Orion, 1998)
(with Ian McDermott)
Mastering the Internet (Orion, 1999)

Ian Shircore can be contacted by e-mail on *shircorebk@aol.com*